New Europe's Old Regions

New Europe's Old Regions

PIOTR ZIENTARA

The Institute of Economic Affairs

First published in Great Britain in 2009 by
The Institute of Economic Affairs
2 Lord North Street
Westminster
London SW1P 3LB
in association with Profile Books Ltd

The mission of the Institute of Economic Affairs is to improve public understanding of the fundamental institutions of a free society, by analysing and expounding the role of markets in solving economic and social problems.

A CIP catalogue record for this book is available from the British Library.

ISBN 978 0 255 36617 5

Many IEA publications are translated into languages other than English or are reprinted. Permission to translate or to reprint should be sought from the Director General at the address above.

Typeset in Stone by MacGuru Ltd
info@macguru.org.uk

Printed and bound in Great Britain by Hobbs the Printers

CONTENTS

THE AUTHOR

Piotr Zientara holds a PhD in Economics (University of Gdansk) and an MA in Human Resource Development (College of Europe in Bruges). He also has a DEUF from University Jean Moulin III in Lyon and an economics diploma from the Paris Chamber of Commerce. He is currently a lecturer in Human Resource Management at Gdansk Higher School of Administration (Department of Social Science and Economics) and a consultant for small and medium-sized enterprises (SMEs). His research interests focus on regional development, industrial relations, labour economics, HR management, sustainable tourism and European integration.

FOREWORD

The recent enlargement of the European Union brought together countries that had dramatically different recent histories. The history of the ex-communist countries that joined the EU had been brutal and the policies adopted by communist governments had been economically disastrous. To a greater or lesser extent, these countries have adopted more open markets, and this has led to some economic improvement.

Despite recent reform, New and Old Europe are marked by huge differences in income levels. As the author shows, particular regions within New Europe have very low productivity, low employment and very low growth. The differences in income levels between EU regions are stark. The income level of the richest EU region is over twelve times the level of that of the poorest. Even ignoring the extremes, which are distorted by special factors, income differences of over threefold between richer and poorer regions are common. To put this in context, these income differences are arguably bigger, for example, than the income differences between the UK and Botswana.

What should be done? Surely, income redistribution on an EU-wide level must be ruled out. There is no intrinsic reason why the poorer regions of the EU cannot become reasonably well off, and surely even the most diehard pro-Europeans could not envisage an EU welfare state. Whatever policies are followed must be oriented towards promoting more widespread prosperity.

The author argues that old-style regional policies will not be helpful here either. They have failed. They rely on government providing subsidies to industries in which the targeted region does not have a comparative advantage.

So what could work? There has been a resurgence of interest in the region as a unit of economic development, and the author gives a moderate welcome to newer types of regional policy. At least these policies are aimed at increasing general levels of productivity rather than subsidising failing industries. EU regional subsidies could also be used to provide infrastructure which, though in principle would be better provided privately, in practice is not generally privately provided in the countries concerned.

In the end, though, regional policy can only be a springboard for considering wider issues. Using Poland as a case study, the author shows how policy must be oriented towards removing government impediments to working and to the establishment of businesses. Employment protection legislation has to be the main target for reform, though social security systems are high on the list too.

The problem is, it appears, that those who are at the centre of decision-making are asking the wrong question. Politicians are asking what they can do for the regions, instead of asking what it is that they currently do which is an impediment to industry and job creation. As ever, labour market regulation penalises and prices out of work the least productive.

The regional problem in the EU must be taken seriously and

the IEA commends this publication as an important contribution to the debate.

PHILIP BOOTH

Editorial and Programme Director,
Institute of Economic Affairs
Professor of Insurance and Risk Management,
Sir John Cass Business School, City University
November 2008

The views expressed in this monograph are, as in all IEA publications, those of the authors and not those of the Institute (which has no corporate view), its managing trustees, Academic Advisory Council or senior staff.

SUMMARY

- Some of the old industrial and agricultural regions of the newly admitted members of the EU are desperately poor by 'Old Europe' standards.

- The richer regions of the EU have twelve times the income levels of the poorest region. Though this is an extreme case, there are many regions of the EU where income levels are just one third of the level enjoyed by a number of richer regions. Income differences within the EU are greater than the income differences between richer EU countries and parts of Africa.

- Conventional regional policy will not close this gap. Policies of 'picking winners' or subsidising industries in which a region does not have a comparative advantage come from precisely the same stable as the sorts of policies that made the regions poor in the first place.

- Low levels of income are also complemented by high levels of unemployment and low levels of productivity. There are tenfold differences between unemployment levels across the EU's regions and twenty-fold differences in productivity levels.

- Such differences, in fact, provide economic opportunities within the context of a free-trade area. Most notably, there is an abundance of low-cost labour in many regions. As has been noted, however, this low-cost labour is also low-productivity labour.

- While traditional regional policy can entrench rather than alleviate these problems, there has been a resurgence of influence in the region as a unit of economic organisation. It is possible that the 'new regionalism' might provide a better route to closing regional income gaps. The new regionalism focuses on raising productivity through education, provision of infrastructure and so on. While large-scale government intervention may not be the best way to achieve these goals, this type of regional intervention is certainly more benign than old-style regional policy.

- The new regionalism can only be the starting point for considering wider issues. Even new approaches to providing regional aid should not be the main thrust of policy. Raising productivity is crucial to raising incomes and employment. This can only happen with substantial market liberalisation – particularly within labour markets.

- A genuine devolution of governmental power to the regions by individual countries is necessary and regions should be given greater responsibility for welfare and labour market policy. Poor regions would then have a strong incentive to reduce impediments to employment, including minimum wages and taxes.

- Poor regions do not have to become centres of innovation and new technology as is often implied in the 'new regionalism'. Comparative advantage may well lie in service industries that employ large amounts of labour that is not especially skilled.

- There are wider lessons for the structure of the EU. If we are to see dynamism and flexibility, as well as the devolution of power, the EU must develop in a way that allows countries to opt out of new legislation. If some countries wish for further integration, they should be content to leave the rest of the EU behind. This will help the process of ensuring that regulation is tailored to the circumstances of a country or region, so that the lack of liberalism in the EU as a whole does not translate into unemployment for New Europe's old regions.

FIGURES, TABLES AND BOXES

AUTHOR'S PREFACE

The entry of the ex-communist countries from central and eastern Europe into the EU in 2004 and 2007 was a truly historic event. The admission of these young democracies put an end to the Yalta-imposed rift that had divided western and eastern Europe for more than five decades. Yet, despite the progress made since the fall of the Berlin Wall, the new entrants to the EU still lag behind their EU-15 counterparts in several respects. There is a big development gap between new and old member states which manifests itself in, among other things, national differences in GDP per capita, poverty rates, labour productivity and the quality of social capital, human resources (HR) and infrastructure. Not only are new entrants less wealthy than old members, but they are also culturally and politically different from them. The ex-communist states, having experienced years of oppression, are naturally more sensitive to all questions related to sovereignty and freedom. Enlargement to the east, therefore, made a far greater impact on the EU's character than any previous accession round. This, in turn, rendered the EU a less homogeneous organisation, thereby necessitating a rethink of its modus operandi.

It is at regional level that the EU's newly acquired heterogeneity comes most conspicuously to the fore. If a new member somehow naturally differs from other countries, its regions – which likewise differ among themselves within the national borders – seem to be even more different from their European counterparts. Hence the enlarged Union's mosaic-like diversity. There are obvious economic differences, at the aggregate level, between countries within the EU. Within countries, there are significant differences between regions. But the differences in the level of economic development between regions of different EU member states are now huge. To put it bluntly, *New Europe contains within it a number of regions that are extremely poor, have low levels of employment and productivity and which are dominated by outdated agricultural and manufacturing industries. These are New Europe's Old Regions.*

All this has profound implications. On the one hand, marked income differentials and high unemployment rates were the driving force behind an unprecedented migration wave after 1 May 2004 (with approximately two million Poles going in search of employment and better prospects to the UK, Ireland and other European countries). On the other hand, the existence of considerable regional disparities in GDP per capita has led to an increase in the amount of money spent by the EU on regional assistance of various forms.

Indeed, the promotion of economic convergence has been Europe's long-standing objective and has brought forth a wide range of structural polices. Nevertheless, it seems that cohesion policy is awkwardly positioned within two overlapping sets of tensions. The first is between distributive and allocative objectives, while the second is between the imperatives of the Lisbon strategy and the demands of convergence in economic activity (Begg, 2008: 8). Is the EU's active regional policy actually inhibiting economic development and productivity growth? This concern reflects more general concerns over the EU's apparently limited capacity to respond to the challenges of a new era.

The old industrial regions of what some have called 'New Europe' have a tendency to exhibit serious poverty and unemployment. Europe's regional policy, at least as currently conceived, may entrench rather than alleviate those problems. We examine this problem mainly in the context of the regional problems faced by Polish regions. In so doing, we address the challenges posed by globalisation and further enlargement, the performance of EU businesses and the rationale of economic liberalisation, the ramifications of European regionalism and its future mode of functioning. Hence the monograph, by focusing on the regional and the central and eastern European dimension, provides an important contribution to the current debate on the condition of the European Union and its need to reinvent itself. Specifically it addresses EU regional policy, something that is a large part of EU spending but rarely discussed in the UK.

The monograph lays great stress on policy implications for Poland, the UK and the EU more generally. It has to be emphasised that, although the monograph focuses chiefly on Poland, the conclusions may well be generally applicable to any country with big regional socio-economic disparities and an active regional policy. It argues, among much else, that, to be truly effective, European regional assistance needs to be combined with free-market reform and, in the Polish context at least, devolution of power from supranational and national government to more local levels. The monograph also makes a case for the EU's enlargement to the east and south, claiming that, for all its flaws, the EU is a groundbreaking project that is highly successful at spreading democracy, stability and prosperity. This does not have any implications, of course, for the desirability or otherwise of any particular state remaining a member of the EU.

1 INTRODUCTION

Old Europe welcomes New Europe

Enlargement of the EU in 2004 marked a turning point in the modern history of Europe. The accession of eight former communist states – the Czech Republic, Estonia, Hungary, Latvia, Lithuania, Poland, Slovakia and Slovenia (plus Malta and Cyprus)[1] – can be regarded as a definite end to the Yalta-imposed division of Europe. When the Iron Curtain fell in 1945 and central and eastern Europe de facto became part of the Soviet empire, it seemed as if the communist regime and the cleavage of the old continent would last for ever (Davies, 1996). All the eight countries had experienced – to varying degrees – political dictatorship, economic mismanagement, technological retardation and degrading poverty. The Baltic republics, having been directly annexed to the USSR, disproportionately bore the brunt of ruthless repression and economic folly. In contrast, Slovenia, as

[1] The present monograph, for the sake of convenience, will use the following abbreviations: the EU-15 – all the old EU member states prior to the 2004 enlargement; the EU-8 – all the new EU member states from central and eastern Europe (without Malta and Cyprus); the EU-10 – the EU-8 plus Malta and Cyprus; the EU-12 – the EU-10 plus Romania and Bulgaria. It is important to make a distinction between the EU-8 and the EU-10 as Malta and Cyprus differ markedly from other countries from central and eastern Europe. Note also that Poland, the Czech Republic, Hungary and Slovakia are sometimes referred to as the Visegrad countries, after the declaration of cooperation they signed in 1991.

Table 1 **EU-27: basic demographic and economic indicators (2007)**

EU country	Population (m)	Area (thousands of square km)	Real GDP growth rate (% change on previous year)	GDP per capita in PPS* (EU-27 = 100)	Labour productivity† (EU-27 = 100)
Austria	8.3	83.9	3.3	130	122.1
Belgium	10.6	30.5	2.1	124	135.4
Bulgaria	7.7	110.9	6.0	39	36.4
Cyprus	0.8	9.3	3.8	94	87.5
Czech Republic	10.3	78.9	5.0	82	73.5
Denmark	5.4	43.1	1.3	126	107.2
Estonia	1.3	45.2	6.4	72	67.3
Finland	5.3	338.1	3.4	118	113.3
France	63.4	544.0	2.0	112	152.5
Germany	82.3	357.0	2.1	114	106.3
Greece	11.2	131.9	3.8	98	118.8
Hungary	10.1	93.0	2.6	65	75.9
Ireland	4.3	70.3	3.5	144	132.9
Italy	59.1	301.3	1.4	103	109.6
Latvia	2.3	64.6	7.2	61	56.7
Lithuania	3.4	65.2	7.5	62	61.6
Luxembourg	0.5	2.6	4.7	284	183.8
Malta	0.4	0.3	3.1	76	88.9

EU country	Population (m)	Area (thousands of square km)	Real GDP growth rate (% change on previous year)	GDP per capita in PPS* (EU-27 = 100)	Labour productivity† (EU-27 = 100)
Netherlands	16.4	41.5	2.7	133	114.2
Poland	38.1	322.6	6.5	55	62.2
Portugal	10.6	91.9	1.8	74	68.3
Romania	21.6	238.4	6.0	39	39.7
Slovakia	5.4	49.0	7.0	68	75.5
Slovenia	2.0	20.3	4.6	92	87.1
Spain	44.5	504.8	3.0	103	100.0
Sweden	9.1	410.9	3.1	124	112.8
United Kingdom	60.9	241.8	3.1	120	112.1
Mean	18.3	158.9	4.0	100.4	96.4
Standard deviation	22.7	157.8	1.8	46.3	33.5

Source: Author's calculations based on: Eurostat (online), available at: http://epp.eurostat.ec.europa.eu/

*Purchasing power standards

†GDP in PPS per person employed

23

the richest part of a Russia-defying Yugoslavia, came out relatively unscathed from the period of communist rule. That said, all the countries of central and eastern Europe were affected by communist ideology, with its negation of market forces and utter disregard for human rights (Mises, 1949; Hayek, 1960; Balcerowicz, 2003).

When the Berlin Wall crumbled in 1989 and the Soviet Union disintegrated two years later, a painful process of transformation from a centrally planned system to a relatively free-market economy began. At the same time, democracy was restored and political pluralism enshrined in the constitutions of the newly born states (Zielonka and Krok-Paszkowska, 2004). The promise of distant (but not unrealistic) European Economic Community (EEC) membership came to be seen as an effective way to consolidate the rule of law and the market mechanism. After many years of strenuous efforts to restore democratic institutions, to entrench market economies and, ultimately, to absorb the *acquis communautaire*, these countries were officially admitted to the EU in 2004. Romania and Bulgaria then joined the EU in January 2007. The process of enlargement is supposed to continue to embrace Albania, Bosnia, Croatia, Serbia, Macedonia and Turkey in the future (Rennie, 2008: 16).

Old Europe and New Europe – economic and political differences

Indeed, the accession of the new members in 2004 (and then in 2007) not only dramatically affected the EU character (Zielonka, 2001) but also proved particularly challenging (Cottrell, 2003: 19). Enlargement from 15 to 27 countries not only increased the

EU's total population to more than 495 million people,[2] but also, even more importantly, reduced a comparatively high degree of western European homogeneity,[3] thereby rendering the EU a less uniform and more loosely knit organisation (see Table 1).

In view of the memories of Soviet rule, the first problem is closely related to the new member states' intrinsic reluctance to cede (part of) their newly regained sovereignty to any supra-national entity[4] and their willingness to maintain strong trans-atlantic ties (Poland was even billed as the USA's Trojan horse in Europe). This stance is viewed with suspicion by the proponents of an 'ever-closer' union. The traditional EU core (mainly France, Belgium, Luxembourg, Italy, Germany and arguably the Nether-lands) aspires – in the name of 'deepening' the Union – both to harmonise the areas of social and economic policy that still fall into the purview of national authorities (taxes, welfare benefits, labour laws) and to reinforce political unity.

The second cause of the EU's increasing heterogeneity is economic in character. Despite noteworthy progress, in terms of GDP per capita the 2004 new entrants still lag far behind the EU-15. The entry of even poorer Romania and Bulgaria threw this issue into particularly sharp focus. But there is another, equally significant, dimension to the economic argument. Given the considerable wage differentials between the west and the east

---

2   With a combined GDP per capita (at PPP) equalling US$28.213 (2007).

3   Arguably, claiming that the EU-15 prior to enlargement was marked by a high de-gree of homogeneity might be an oversimplification; indeed, there have existed remarkable cultural and socio-economic differences among 'Old Europe' coun-tries since the very beginning of the integration processes. Nevertheless, as seen from the perspective of the Soviet bloc, they constituted a more or less homo-geneous grouping adhering to the principles of democracy and capitalism.

4   This attitude is illustrated by the typical slogan of central and eastern European eurosceptics: 'In the past it was Moscow that called the tune, now it is Brussels'.

of the EU, the accession countries – offering low-cost labour, a business-friendly climate and a continually growing market potential – have become especially attractive to foreign and other EU investors. With the progressive dismantling of barriers to the free flow of capital and labour,[5] and the rapid propagation of information and communication technologies (ICTs), many EU-15 (as well as US and Asian) companies have decided to shift production and outsource office tasks to EU-12 countries. Also, thousands of central and eastern Europeans – mostly highly skilled manual workers and university graduates – have gone in search of employment to the UK, Ireland and other EU-15 member states.

These processes provoked a backlash in many EU-15 countries and prompted emotional protests against various stereotypes: (i) Polish plumbers stealing French jobs; (ii) national companies betraying compatriots and shifting production (hence axeing local jobs) to lower-cost Slovakia or Estonia; (iii) central and eastern European governments introducing free-market reforms and pursuing a sort of 'beggar-thy-neighbour' policy vis-à-vis their western counterparts, thus striking at the heart of (peculiarly understood) European unity. Hence it is argued that the EU is currently undergoing a sort of identity crisis – a presupposition that was reinforced by French and Dutch voters' rejection of the

5   The principle of free flow of goods, services, workers and capital, being enshrined in the successive European treaties, constitutes the fundamental 'pillar' of the EU. That said, there is no doubt that barriers to free flow still exist. This takes the form of: (1) restrictions on labour mobility (in 2007 seven EU-15 member states still kept their markets shut for workers from central and eastern Europe) and (2) attempts by national governments (chiefly France, Germany and Spain, but also Poland) to thwart takeovers of so-called national 'treasures' by foreign companies.

draft constitutional treaty in 2005, and the Irish 'no' to the Treaty of Lisbon in 2008.

A Europe of regions?

The implications of the economic argument are central to this monograph. Marked GDP per capita differentials, higher-than-average poverty rates and other socio-economic disproportions, together with the dilemmas associated with liberal reform, structural change and development aid, are most illustrative when looked at from the regional perspective. It is at regional level that the disparities between the west of the EU and the east are particularly conspicuous. In other words, even though central and eastern European countries have become richer on aggregate and have thus reduced the distance to their western neighbours (European Commission, 2007b), regional disparities within the enlarged EU seem to be diminishing at a slower pace. Some regions of new member states are desperately poor. More generally, most new member states are marked by persisting urban–rural, core–periphery divides.

But it is also at regional level that the consequences of enlargement (and globalisation in general) are most intensely experienced by the citizens of the EU-15. As deindustrialisation – boosted by restructuring processes, which involve relocation of production and outsourcing of business functions – gathers momentum, many traditional (industry-dominated) and/or peripheral regions in 'Old' Europe have seen jobs disappear and reconversion efforts slow down (OECD, 2006: 30). The regional perspective seems even more pertinent in view of the emphasis the EU places on its cohesion policy (Leonardi, 2005), which, governed by Articles 2 and 4, and Title XVII of the Treaty Establishing the European Community (TEC), accounts for 25 per cent of the EU budget (Esposti, 2008: 14).

Indeed, as has been noted, the promotion of economic convergence has been the EU's long-standing objective. In practice, economic and social cohesion is defined in terms of reducing regional disparities as measured by GDP per head (relative to the EU average) in PPP terms. In consequence, a wide array of structural policies has been in place since the late 1980s, the impact of which on the process of convergence among European regions is subject to much debate (De Michelis, 2008; Esposti, 2008). In this context, it is important to note that the Lisbon Treaty (assuming it is adopted) will somehow modify the definition of cohesion through the addition of the word 'territorial', 'implying a focus on spatial balance in economic development' (Begg, 2008: 3).

How EU regional policy can work against the Lisbon Agenda

Since the relaunch (in 2005) of the Lisbon Strategy – whose overarching (and unrealistic) objective is to turn Europe into the most competitive economy in the world by 2010 – structural polices have been supposed not only to reduce regional differences, but also to enhance the EU's aggregate competitiveness. Indeed, the European Commission (2007b) highlights that cohesion policy is confluent with the goals of the Lisbon Strategy by promoting growth and employment. Yet this assertion is highly problematic. For one thing, regional policy is regarded primarily as a distributive policy whose 'supply-side' effects on growth are at best hard to evaluate (Esposti, 2008: 15; Begg, 2008: 7–8) and, for another, it allocates resources to areas where they are less productive, which is in principle in conflict with the promotion of growth (Santos, 2008).

On the other hand, the shift to a knowledge-based economy (Smith, 2000; Dolfsma, 2008) has coincided with the resurgence of interest in the region as a scale of economic organisation (Scott, 1996, 1998; Storper, 1997; Armstrong and Taylor, 2000). Proximity-facilitated innovation generation, technology diffusion underpinned by knowledge spillovers, social-capital-lubricated collaboration and networking-driven inter-cluster cooperation have all come to be seen as vital elements of regional development strategies (see, *inter alia*, Simmie, 1997, 2003; Cooke and Morgan, 1998; European Commission, 2007c; Breschi and Malerba, 2005; Cumbers and MacKinnon, 2005; Porter, 2007; Dolfsma, 2008). Much hope has also been pinned on the capacity of ICT to transform the fortunes of disadvantaged, remote regions (Cornford et al., 1996; OECD, 2001b). Furthermore, the concept of the learning region[6] – shifting the focus from R&D activity and technological progress to institutional and cultural factors – has offered novel insights into the mechanisms of regional economies (Lundvall and Johnson, 1994; Morgan 1997; Maskell and Törnqvist, 1999).

This finds its reflection in the EU's documents. In the integrated guidelines for the Lisbon Strategy, innovation poles or clusters are mentioned in Guideline 8, which refers to 'helping to bridge the technology gap between regions'. Likewise, Guideline 10 centres on networking between clusters (Begg, 2008: 4). Yet doubts are currently being cast both over the new regionalism's ability to deliver the processes it promises as well as over whether

---

6   It was even hailed as a 'revolution' in regional thinking (Armstrong and Taylor, 2000: 292).

development processes are actually as critical to the spatial workings of the economy as the new paradigm assumes (Hudson 1999; Lovering, 1999; MacKinnon et al., 2002; Martin and Sunley, 2003; Purcell, 2004). In a similar vein, it is increasingly clear that many of the supposed benefits of ICT have failed to materialise (cf. Jæger and Storgaard 1997; Clark, 2001; Gillespie et al., 2001; Schmied, 2002). That said, as will be demonstrated later on, these reservations should not be uncritically accepted either.

New Europe's old industrial regions

Regional differences in incomes exist in most developed countries.[7] Nevertheless, from a purely pragmatic conservative perspective, they ought not to be too conspicuous and disproportionate.[8] This is because conspicuous income disproportions risk upsetting the delicate social balance and, in turn, risk undermining the capitalist framework in a democracy. In ex-communist countries at the very beginning of the transformation entire professional groups got impoverished, while ex-apparatchiks-turned-democrats used their connections to seize opportunities offered by the advent of capitalism and the yawning gaps in the law resulting from the

7 Just as some people will always be more affluent than others because of differences in: (1) skill (human capital); (2) approach to work and leisure; (3) propensity to save (and invest); (4) size of family and life expectancy, we can expect these differences to exist between the average incomes of people grouped by region.

8 Of course, one might justifiably ask how we tell what is 'too' much difference. We do not make such a value judgement here. It is worth noting, however, that, if the government of a particular country guarantees a particular minimum level of income through the social security system and large numbers of people in a given region cannot achieve a level of income greater than that minimum through employment, then there are going to be lasting differences between employment levels in different regions.

inexperience of the early reformers. This, in turn, provoked an anti-capitalist backlash and a yearning for the comeback of equality-imposing 'good socialist times'.

From a more economically liberal perspective, if regional differences exist because of interventionist policies that hold back particular regions, then this is unambiguously bad policy.

Equally significantly, by focusing on the regional agenda in central and eastern Europe, the monograph attempts to address issues of general interest to the entire European project. Thus it both examines through the prism of New Europe's regionalism the rationale of the EU regional development agenda (its cohesion policy and its apparent drive for innovation and competitiveness) and comes up with concrete policy recommendations designed to improve the situation in disadvantaged EU-12 regions.

The monograph chiefly focuses on Poland, contrasting its regional experience with that of other EU countries (both old and new members). This approach takes as its premise the presupposition that Poland, the biggest new member state,[9] which is endowed with sizeable regions and an increasingly uncompetitive and business-unfriendly economy (Heritage Foundation, 2008; World Bank, 2008; World Economic Forum, 2008a, 2008b), can serve as an illustration of certain processes and phenomena typical, to varying degrees, of all EU countries – but especially the new entrants.

9   Poland accounts for roughly 50 per cent of the EU-10 population and 40 per cent of its GDP. In 2006 – that is, prior to the accession of Romania and Bulgaria – it was the poorest EU-25 member state (with the EU-25 equalling 100, its GDP per capita at PPP stood at 52.3).

Summary

The monograph proceeds as follows. Chapter 2 presents statistical data for EU-27 regions to provide a background against which to discuss general regional issues. Chapter 3 then examines how enlargement to the east has affected the EU's character and functioning. It explores the economic and political ramifications of the accession of the ex-communist countries for the entire Community and individual member states. In this context, we discuss the condition of European business and the structural weaknesses of the EU economy. In further chapters, we then discuss the implications of European regionalism and the wider framework of EU cohesion policy and analyse the challenges posed to the regions by globalisation and EU integration.

Chapter 6 discusses the discourses and doctrines associated with the new regionalism, placing special emphasis on the concept of the 'learning' region and the importance of social capital. Chapter 7 then uses Poland as a case study. Specifically, it discusses the transformation of the Polish economy, examines the problem of lack of social capital, and contrasts its performance with that of other central and eastern European countries.

Chapters 8 to 10 focus on important policy issues. First, we examine 'non-solutions': that is, regional and other policies which ought to be avoided. Then we examine the effectiveness of EU cohesion policy. The main proposal is for a strategy combining economic liberalisation and further decentralisation with the fundamental premises of the new regionalism. The key to success in reducing regional differences is the ability for continual change and adaptation as well as cooperation between local actors: this cannot happen without liberalisation. This leads into a discussion of the EU's *raison d'être* and its regional agenda. We argue that the

EU should allow 'coalitions of the willing' combined with further enlargement. This is more likely to lead to openness and diversity rather than the harmonisation-driven uniformity that results from the current approach.

2 REGIONAL DISPARITIES AT EU AND MEMBER STATE LEVEL

It is between regions rather than between countries that the differences in the level of economic development in the EU are particularly manifested. Indeed, many of the central and eastern European capital regions are thriving and are soon likely to catch up with the EU-27. Accordingly, the emphasis here is placed on growing urban–rural, core–periphery divisions within the EU-12. The problem is not so much regional disparities per se, however. Rather, it is stagnation and non-functioning labour markets in certain areas which pose the main challenge.

The EU is a unique alliance of markedly different nation-states undergoing a process of integration. Its uniqueness stems from the fact that nominally independent countries voluntarily agree to cede part of their sovereignty in the name of the overarching aim of European unity. It follows that in the eyes of most Europeans (or at least their democratically elected governments) the benefits of joining the EU outweigh the potential disadvantages associated with the loss of independence. Never before has a project of comparable scope and vision been carried through (see also Davies, 1996).

Both from the perspective of an individual country and from that of the entire EU, the decision to apply for membership and then the accession itself are heavy with implications. The obligation to meet all the membership criteria dramatically affects a candidate country's functioning, while the need to accommodate a new member might entail a rethink of the existing procedures and policies within the EU itself. Furthermore, the entry of a new country invariably brings with it its own peculiar problems and unique cultural heritage, which risks decreasing the EU's homogeneity, thereby making it a less closely knit grouping.

But there is a significant regional dimension to the accession process, so enlargement makes a profound impact both on the regional agenda of a member state and on the EU. Not only does a new entrant naturally differ in some respects from other members, but also its regions – which likewise differ among themselves within the national boundaries – will be different from other EU regions. If there are noticeable regional differences within Spain – say, between Andalusia and Navarra – it seems likely that the differences will be even more pronounced between (say) Andalusia and the Polish region of Lubelskie. They will be mainly of linguistic, cultural and historical character (we will explore the ramifications of European regionalism for the standing of national governments in Chapter 4).

This pan-European regional diversity also manifests itself in the area of economics, taking the form of regional disparities in terms of GDP per capita, income, unemployment rates or labour productivity.[1] Enlargement to the east indeed contributed to widening disparities within the EU both at national and regional levels (Eurostat, 2007: 26; Begg, 2008: 3). Yet it is at regional level that the differences are most conspicuous (Eurostat, 2006: 33). In 2004, for instance, GDP per head was almost five times higher in the top 10 per cent of regions (ranked by GDP per capita) than in

---

1   Regional economic disparities exist in most modern states, well-developed and less prosperous countries alike (OECD, 2005).

the bottom 10 per cent (Eurostat, 2007: 26). Moreover, as will be demonstrated when analysing Poland's regional agenda, considerable disproportions exist within the regions themselves, normally resulting from an urban–rural, core–periphery dichotomy. It is instructive, therefore, to examine statistical data for 268 EU regions, placing special emphasis on the situation in central and eastern Europe.[2]

We thus look at basic socio-economic indicators such as GDP/income per capita, employment/unemployment rates, labour productivity and productivity growth. The values of these indicators, giving a picture of both regional wealth and the situation in the local labour market, illustrate not only the level of the general development of a given region, but also the living standards of its inhabitants.

GDP per capita

We first analyse the regional distribution of GDP per head (2003) in purchasing power standards (PPS), as calculated by Eurostat

---

2   Note that all statistics at regional level within the EU are based on the nomenclature of territorial units for statistics (NUTS). It was established by Eurostat more than thirty years ago in order to provide a single uniform breakdown of territorial units for the production of regional statistics for the EU. In each member state, a three-level hierarchy of regions – NUTS1, NUTS2 and NUTS3 – was established on the basis of existing administrative regions or groupings of these. Regions at NUTS level 1 are large subnational units (such as Scotland or Bavaria), each of which usually comprises a number of NUTS2 regions (such as *comunidades autónomas* in Spain or *voivodships* in Poland). In turn, these are made up of NUTS3 regions (such as the *Kreis* in Germany). Fundamentally, regional analysis in this section is based on the NUTS2 classification. This means that in some countries the number of NUTS regions corresponds with the number of official administrative units (Poland) or, more frequently, that it does not (for instance, in the case of the UK).

Table 2 **Some EU-15 and EU-12 regions (GDP per capita in PPS, 2003)**

Region	Country	Place	GDP per capita
Inner London	The UK	1	60,342
Brussels	Belgium	2	51.658
Luxembourg	Grand Duchy of Luxembourg	3	50,844
Hamburg	Germany	4	40,011
Île de France	France	5	37,687
Prague	Czech Republic	19	30,052
Bratislavsky Kraj	Slovakia	53	25,190
Közép Magyarország	Hungary	130	20,627
Slovenia	Slovenia	190	16,527
Mazowieckie	Poland	203	15,833
Malta	Malta	204	15,797
Nord-Est	Romania	268	4,721

Source: Eurostat (2006: 27–8)

(2006: 27). This indicator offers a simple yardstick of regional prosperity. By this gauge, Inner London is the richest region in the EU-27 (PPS 60,342), whereas Nord-Est in Romania is the poorest region (PPS 4,721). Brussels (PPS 51,658) and Luxembourg (PPS 50,844) follow in second and third places (see Table 2). It is worth noting the very high standing of Prague (nineteenth place) – the region with the highest GDP per capita in the new member states (PPS 30,052). Yet the Czech capital is an exception among the EU-12 regions, which lag far behind.[3] Altogether, in 74 of the 268 EU-27 regions, the per capita GDP in PPS in 2003 was less than 75

3   Botswana's GDP per head in 2001 (US$3,832) is higher than that of the Polish region of Lubelskie (approximately US$3,620), which – prior to the accession of Romania and Bulgaria – was the poorest region in the entire EU, in the same year. Note that the above GDP per capita values are *not* calculated on a PPP basis.

per cent of the EU-25 average. As might be expected, most of those regions are situated in new member states as well as in eastern Germany and in the southern and western periphery of the EU-15.

At the upper end of the spectrum, 36 regions had a per capita GDP of more than 125 per cent of the EU-25 average in 2003. Most of these affluent regions are in southern Germany, in the south of the UK, in northern Italy, in northern Belgium and in Luxembourg, the Netherlands, Ireland and Scandinavia. Madrid, Paris and, most interestingly, Prague also fell into this category.

There are also substantial regional differences within the EU countries themselves. In the EU-15, the largest regional differences are in the UK and Belgium. By contrast, the lowest values are in Sweden and in Ireland. But conspicuous regional differences in GDP per head are a characteristic of the EU-12 countries. Also worth noting is that in all the new member states and in a number of the old ones, a considerable share of economic activity is concentrated in the capital regions. Certainly, it is in the capital regions that the highest per capita GDP is generated. Hence, with the notable exceptions of Berlin and Rome, the regions of Brussels, Prague, Madrid, Paris, Lisbon, Budapest, Bratislava, London, Sofia and Bucharest occupy a prominent position in national economies.

In 1999–2003 the process of catching up – in terms of a region's per capita GDP – was concentrated in the EU's peripheral areas, both in the EU-15 and the EU-12 countries. Among the former, it was Greece, Spain, Ireland and the UK where economic growth was strongest. Other EU-15 peripheral states, however, such as Italy and Portugal, did not experience comparable economic dynamism: no Italian and Portuguese region (except for Madeira) achieved the average growth of the EU-25. The same can be said about Germany and France, where most of the regions also fell short of the EU average in terms of economic growth. In sharp contrast to the European core, many regions in the EU-12 countries experienced above-average growth. This happened in the capital regions of the Baltic republics, Slovenia, Hungary, Bulgaria and Romania. The biggest disappointment was Poland, where the regional increases in GDP per capita values were only slightly above the EU-25 average (despite the low level of GDP overall).

Nord-Est, in Romania, was the non-capital EU-12 region with the strongest growth. Its GDP per capita in PPS increased by 6.7 percentage points in 1999–2003 from 22.4 per cent to 29.1 per cent of the EU-25 average. The Portuguese region of Norte was the least prosperous in the EU-15. Norte's GDP per head (57.4 per cent of the EU average) was exactly the same as that of the Romanian capital, Bucharest.

On average, the new member states seem to be catching up with the EU-25 average at a rate of 0.8 percentage points every year, which, at first sight, seems to bode well for the future in terms of reducing regional differences in income. It transpires on closer inspection, however, that not all EU-12 regions followed the pattern of dynamic growth. This applies in particular to Poland, Malta, Cyprus and, to some degree, the Czech Republic and Bulgaria. By and large, 24 of the 55 regions in the new member states grew by fewer than 3 percentage points, which was below the average. Of those 24 regions, twelve were in Poland, six in the Czech Republic and three in Bulgaria. Worryingly, six regions fell even farther behind: four in Poland, one in Bulgaria and one in Romania.[4]

---

4   The dynamics of economic development across the regions in one country can diverge almost as widely as between regions in different countries. The most

Income

As Eurostat (2007: 36) observes, GDP per capita in PPS has a number of drawbacks as an indicator of regional wealth. One of them is that a 'place-of work' figure (the GDP produced in the region) is divided by a 'place-of-residence' figure (the population living in the region). This inconsistency is relevant whenever there are commuter flows (more or fewer people working in a region than living in it), as with the Inner London region. Equally, other factors can cause the regional distribution of actual income not to correspond to the distribution of GDP. These include, for instance, income from rent, interest or dividends obtained by the residents of a certain region, but paid by the residents of other regions.[5]

In 2004 the centres of prosperity – with primary income of private households per inhabitant above 18,000 PPCS (purchasing power consumption standards) – were to be found, *inter alia*, in southern England, Paris and Alsace, northern Italy, Vienna, Madrid, Flanders, the western Netherlands, Stockholm, Bayern and Baden Württemberg (Eurostat, 2007: 36). One can

conspicuous differences in dynamics can be seen in the Netherlands and Romania, where the per capita GDP in the most economically dynamic regions increased by around 20 percentage points more than in the least. The corresponding figures for the UK and Portugal were 17 and 15 percentage points respectively. At the opposite end of the spectrum lie Sweden and Belgium, with a regional range of 8 percentage points. The glaring regional differences within the new member states can be put down largely to the dynamic growth of the capital regions.

5   In the text, a distinction will be made between the primary and secondary income as well as the disposable income of private households (for the exact definitions, see Eurostat, 2006: 39). Owing to lack of data, Cyprus, Luxembourg, Malta, Slovenia and Bulgaria, as well as the Autonomous Provinces of Bolzano and Trento (Italy), and the French Overseas Departments, are not included in the analysis in this section.

also notice a clear north–south divide in Italy and a west–east one in Germany. To a lesser extent, a south–north divide is also visible in the UK and Belgium. Household *primary* income in the new member states lay considerably below the EU average. Only the capital regions – Prague, Mazowieckie (Poland), Közép Magyarország (Hungary) and Bucharest – found themselves within the 6,000–12,000 PPCS range. The eastern peripheral regions of some of the new member states were even farther behind the respective national level, giving a clear west–east division not only in Poland but also in Romania and Slovakia.

As with the GDP per capita values, the least affluent region on an income per head basis was Nord-Est in Romania (2,696 PPCS), whereas the wealthiest one was the UK region of Inner London (29,411 PPCS). The ten regions with the highest per capita income included five regions in the UK, three in Germany and one each in France and Belgium. A comparison of primary income with disposable income highlights the levelling impact of state intervention (income redistribution). Government-conducted redistribution increases the relative income level in southern Italy, central and southern Spain, the west and the north in the UK, and in parts of eastern Germany and central Greece. Redistribution also levels disposable income across the regions in the new member states. Yet the levelling out of private income levels in New Europe was generally less manifest than in Old Europe. And, despite state intervention, the capital regions maintain their edge over the periphery. At 11,038 PPCS per head, Közép Magyarország was the region with the highest disposable income in the accession countries (followed closely by Prague, which came top in 2003).

State activity reduced the ratio between the highest and the lowest regional value from a factor of 10.9 to 6.9. The largest regional disparity in wealth within a given country – a factor of 2.05 – can be observed in Romania. Income in the Bucharest region was more than double that in Nord-Est. Poland had the lowest income disparity among the new member states. Yet, given the potentially insidious effects of the government intervention that results in increases in regional *disposable* income (Smith, 2006: 119–37), this does not have to be interpreted as a positive aspect. In the EU-15 the smallest regional income disparities (11–32 per cent) were to be found in Ireland, Austria, the Netherlands and Sweden.

In this context, it might be instructive to compare Ireland and Poland (a comparison frequently made in the Polish literature). The latter country had the lowest income disparity in the EU-12, the former in the EU-15. Poland was also the country with the largest number of regions (thirteen out of sixteen) in which disposable income exceeds the primary income (which suggests a high degree of income redistribution).[6] Ireland, in sharp contrast to Poland, has the lowest GDP per capita disparity (a factor of 1.6) in the entire Community. This may imply that in Ireland wealth is generated in a more or less uniform way all over the country. That is not the case in Poland, where only a few core regions experience above-average economic growth and end up subsidising the less affluent periphery (mainly in eastern Poland).

6　Apart from monetary social benefits from the state, other transfer payments too – for instance, remittances from abroad or other regions – can cause disposable income to exceed primary income. Prior to 2004 many Poles worked illegally in the EU-15 and the money they sent home may have contributed to the increase in disposable income. In Poland intra-national labour mobility, unlike transnational labour mobility (witness the mass exodus of Polish workers to the UK and Ireland after 1 May 2004), is generally low, so transfers from people working in other Polish regions had no significant effect on regional disposable income.

Employment and unemployment rates

The EU as a whole compares unfavourably with the USA in terms of unemployment and employment levels: the average joblessness rate in the EU is roughly twice as high as in the USA. With the accession of the central and eastern European countries in 2004, labour market statistics were not improved as some of the new entrants – notably Poland – were plagued by very high unemployment. In some Polish regions unemployment exceeded 25 per cent and in many subregions it even topped 35 per cent.[7] Hence again it is at regional level that disparities seem to be most conspicuous. It might be informative to look at labour market indicators from the regional perspective so as to see the magnitude and causes of the differences, and hence to understand the nature of the problems facing many EU regions, especially those situated in the EU-12 countries.

In 2004 the employment rate at EU level stood at 63.1 per cent compared with 62.8 per cent in 2003. At national level, Denmark (75.5 per cent), Sweden (72.1 per cent) and the UK (71.6 per cent) were the countries with the highest employment rate (yet, given high hidden unemployment in Sweden, one should treat its second place with suspicion). Malta (54.1 per cent) and Poland (51.7 per cent) found themselves at the other end of the spectrum.[8] Regions with an employment rate of over 67 per cent can be found in Belgium (the central region of Vlaams-Brabant), the Netherlands (all twelve regions), the UK (31 out of 37 regions), the Czech Republic (the capital region of Prague and the central region of Střední Čechy) and Slovakia (the capital region of Bratislava).

---

7 Unemployment fell to 9.3 per cent in September 2008. This was due, however, to mass emigration to Britain and Ireland rather than to any supply-side reform.

8 Poland's employment rate was, therefore, the lowest in the entire Community.

By contrast, rates below 55 per cent were recorded in 42 regions; these included: five in Spain, seven in southern Italy, four in Hungary, two in Slovakia and as many as fourteen out of sixteen regions in Poland.

In 2004 the unemployment rate in the EU was 9.2 per cent. At regional level, the worst situation was observed in Polish and east German regions (see Table 3), where unemployment exceeded 20 per cent. In Romania unemployment was far lower, ranging from 6.2 per cent (Nord-Est) to 9.9 per cent (Sud-Est). The unemployment rate in Inner London in the UK is around 3 per cent compared with 28 per cent in Warmińsko-Mazurskie in Poland. Clearly, the regional disparities in unemployment levels are much more conspicuous than those in GDP or income per head.

Table 3 **Selected regions with lowest and highest unemployment (2004)**

Regions with lowest unemployment			Regions with highest unemployment		
Region	Country	Rate (%)	Region	Country	Rate (%)
Åland	Finland	2.6	Warmińsko-Mazurskie	Poland	27.8
Nord Est	Italy	3.2	Zachodniopomorskie	Poland	25.8
Oost Nederland	The Netherlands	3.5	Lubuskie	Poland	25.6
South-East	The UK	3.8	Mecklenburg	(East) Germany	20.1
Közép Magyarország	Hungary	4.0	Sachsen Anhalt	(East) Germany	19.6

Sources: Eurostat (2006); Office for National Statistics; Central Statistical Office (2004), *Statistical Yearbook* 2003, Warsaw

Labour productivity and productivity growth

Regional differences in labour productivity are even larger than those in unemployment rates. To begin with, there is a fairly clear-cut west–east division line. Western Europe (with the notable exception of some regions in Italy and Portugal) is characterised by far higher labour productivity than the ex-communist countries of central and eastern Europe. This, of course, is the legacy of the communist past, when the absence of market forces – coupled with crass mismanagement, technological backwardness, a socialist work ethos and the substandard quality of human resource management – all resulted in extremely low labour productivity. There is no doubt that increasing labour productivity is the key to fast economic growth and hence higher living standards. It is one of the main challenges faced by the EU-12 in the near future.

In 2004, for instance, more than €80,000 per person employed – to use one possible gauge of productivity – was generated in southern and eastern Ireland, the Grand Duchy of Luxembourg, the Île-de-France region and Brussels. By contrast, less than €10,000 per person employed was generated in all Bulgarian and Romanian regions (apart from Bucharest). As might be expected, labour productivity was also very high (over €60,000 per person employed) in other regions of Old Europe (Vlaams-Brabant, Alsace, Oberbayern), as well as in large urban areas such as Inner London, Stockholm or Hamburg. Nevertheless, there are vast interregional differences in labour productivity within individual EU-15 countries. Predictably, owing to the reunification, this is the case in Germany (a maximum difference of €32,897 per person employed), but also in the UK (a maximum difference of €28,420 per person employed).

Not surprisingly, labour productivity in all regions of new

member states was much lower than in old member states. Except for Slovenia, Prague and Közép Magyarország in Hungary, in 2003, it was below €20,000 per person employed. Considerable progress was made, however, even before the EU-12 joined the EU. Particularly high labour productivity growth rates were recorded in the Baltic states (1998–2003), in all regions of Poland (Świętokrzyskie had the highest rate of growth of output per employed person, a rise of 55 per cent over the same period) and in some regions of Slovakia and the Czech Republic.

As Eurostat (2006: 72–3) itself admits, calculating labour productivity per person employed does not take into consideration the differing lengths of working time and the extent of part-time employment. So it is more instructive to look at labour productivity figures calculated on the basis of hours of work performed. Table 4 shows the ten best- and worst-performing regions in the EU with respect to labour productivity calculated in this way. It emerges that, if the calculation of labour productivity is based on hours worked, the aforesaid west–east productivity division is magnified. There is, in other words, a huge gap between the region of Groningen in the Netherlands, where productivity is highest (€52.6 per hour), and Nord-Est in Romania, where productivity is only €1.9 euro per hour (see Table 4).

Admittedly, the productivity gap is reducing as productivity in the countries where it is low (the EU-12) is growing at a higher rate than in the countries where it is high (the EU-15). This, in turn, is the result of a combination of context-specific factors. These include: (1) ex-communist governments' reformist efforts; (2) integration-driven inflows of capital (in the form of foreign direct investment) to the new member states; (3) pre-accession and post-accession regional EU aid used by regional authorities

Table 4 **Labour productivity per hour worked: best- and worst-performing regions in the EU-27 (2003)**

	Regions with highest productivity (euro per hour)			Regions with lowest productivity (euro per hour)		
Region	Country	Euro per hour	Region	Country	Euro per hour	
Groningen	The Netherlands	52.6	Nord-Vest	Romania	2.8	
Luxembourg	Luxembourg	49.6	Yugoiztochen	Bulgaria	2.7	
Southern & eastern	Ireland	48.1	Severozapaden	Bulgaria	2.7	
Île-de-France	France	48.0	Sud-Est	Romania	2.6	
Hamburg	Germany	45.4	Severoiztochen	Bulgaria	2.6	
Brussels	Belgium	44.5	Severen tsentralen	Bulgaria	2.6	
Stockholm	Sweden	42.3	Sud	Romania	2.5	
Oberbayern	Germany	42.1	Yuzhen tsentralen	Bulgaria	2.5	
Utrecht	The Netherlands	41.6	Sud-Vest	Romania	2.3	
Darmstadt	Germany	41.5	Nord-Est	Romania	1.9	

Source: Eurostat (2006: 74)

Table 5 **Best-performing and worst-performing EU regions**

Indicator	Best-performing regions			Worst-performing regions		
	Region	Country	Value	Region	Country	Value
GDP per capita (PPS in % of EU-27 average) (2005)	Inner London	UK	302.7	Nord-Est	Romania	24.2
	Luxembourg	Luxembourg	264.3	Severozapaden	Bulgaria	26.9
	Hamburg	Germany	202.1	Severen tsentralen	Bulgaria	26.9
Unemployment (%) (2007)	Zeeland	The Netherlands	2.1	Meklenburg-Vorpommeren	Germany	17.4
	The region of Prague	The Czech Rep.	2.4	Leipzig	Germany	17.2
	Bolzano-Bozen	Italy	2.6	The region of Brussels	Belgium	17.1
Labour productivity (euro per hour) (2003)	Groningen	The Netherlands	52.6	Nord-Vest	Romania	2.8
	Luxembourg	Luxembourg	49.6	Yugoiztochen	Bulgaria	2.7
	Southern & eastern Ireland		48.1	Severozapaden	Bulgaria	2.7

Sources: Eurostat (2008), *Regional Statistics*, available at: http://epp.eurostat.ec.europa.eu/; Eurostat (2006: 74)

for human resources and technology upgrading as well as infrastructure development. All those issues will be discussed below.

In the light of the above analysis, it is clear that there still exist vast regional disparities within the enlarged EU. The differences in unemployment and labour productivity levels between EU regions are particularly conspicuous. Even though one can observe substantial differences in terms of basic socio-economic indicators within some of the EU-15 countries (north–south in Italy or west–east in Germany) as well as in some of the EU-12 countries (west–east in Poland and Romania), it is between EU-15 regions and EU-12 regions that disparities are at their most acute. There now exists one economic union within which there are huge disparities between the economic performance and wellbeing of different areas. The description above has used a number of statistics, mainly taken from the time of accession of the new members. In Table 5, the extreme regional differentials are brought out by showing the three most successful regions and the three least successful regions by each of GDP per capita, unemployment rates and labour productivity. The most recently published consistent data are used in each case.

Despite the noteworthy progress made by most central and eastern European regions (especially the capital region of Prague) since 1989, the west–east division line is likely to characterise Europe's spatial distribution of income wealth for some time in the future. Yet, with EU-12 metropolitan areas facing bright developmental prospects, this might be accompanied by the emergence of another division line that would take the form of core–periphery, urban–rural divisions running across eastern Europe. The aggregate performance of the EU-12 may well hide the dire performance of substantial regions within the EU-12.

3 ECONOMIC AND POLITICAL STRUCTURE OF EUROPE

The chapter examines the impact that enlargement to the east has made on the character and functioning of the EU. It explores the economic and political ramifications of the accession of the ex-communist countries for the entire Community and for individual member states. In this context, we discuss the condition of European business and the structural weaknesses of the EU economy.

Economic and political ramifications

The demise of communism in 1989 ushered in a new era of European integration: the fall of the Iron Curtain put an end to the Yalta-imposed division of the old continent into two hostile blocks. The process was further bolstered by the accession of eight former Soviet satellites into the EU in 2004. The ex-communist countries voluntarily pledged to abide by the standards of democracy and, even more remarkably, agreed to cede part of their newly regained sovereignty to a supranational institution (Zielonka and Krok-Paszkowska, 2004). Yet not only did they become fully fledged EU members on a par with well-established democracies such as Britain or France, but they also brought with them a 'scent' of utter penury as well as experience and values not always understood in the West.

As a result of enlargement to the east, the EU is now characterised by a far higher degree of heterogeneity than in the not-so-distant past. This is discernible in both the political and economic dimensions. Politically, the homogeneity of the Union is likely to be challenged by the newcomers' strong ties with the USA, as already exemplified by the decision of Poland and the Baltic republics to send their troops to help the Americans fight in Iraq and by their understandable mistrust of Russia. This is bound to run counter to the anti-American and pro-Russian instincts of the European core of France and Germany.

In the newly restored democracies of central and eastern Europe, politics is also plagued by immaturity and instability, sometimes a consequence of adopting proportional representation. This often brings forth politicians who have few inhibitions and who defy the EU tradition of reaching a compromise at all costs. Once on the European stage, they are undiplomatically outspoken and resort to the veto threat if their interests are jeopardised. In this regard, Poland is widely seen as the 'EU troublemaker-in chief'. The country voiced its opposition to German–Russian plans to build a gas pipeline in the Baltic Sea and blocked the signing of a new EU–Russia trade agreement in 2007 because of Russia's embargo on Polish meat (when the embargo was finally lifted in late 2007, Poland gave up its veto).

Economically, enlargement has affected the EU's homogeneity even more dramatically, widening intra-EU national disparities far more than during previous accessions. The Community incorporated countries that not only are markedly poorer (see Table 1 in Chapter 1) than old members, but also have different economic structures, with many people still employed in manufacturing and agriculture. The process of convergence in average income per person is likely to take decades. The EU now comprises both well-developed high-income countries such as Sweden and the UK and middle-income countries such as Poland or Bulgaria (interestingly, the combined GDP of the EU-10 is only about 25 per cent of the UK's GDP alone).

Yet such economic heterogeneity has far-reaching implications. First, new members offer low-cost labour, which attracts EU-15 companies seeking to cut production costs through relocation and outsourcing. But cheap labour also acts as a magnet for American or Asian businesses. Lured by a growing market potential and, above all, by the opportunity to establish a foothold for further expansion in the entire EU, they increasingly tend to favour the EU-12 over the EU-15 when making location decisions.

The competition for international capital is seen in some old member states as unfair. This is compounded by the fact that most EU-12 countries have been more successful in implementing free-market reforms and offer a more friendly investor environment than most old members. For instance, several new entrants not only introduced flat-tax regimes, but also cut red tape and made labour markets more flexible (World Bank, 2008). This overall business friendliness, coupled with low-cost labour, more than offsets low (but rising) labour productivity in the new EU countries.

This all risks giving rise to intra-EU tensions. Proponents of further integration ('ever-closer' union) who see in the (upward) harmonisation of taxes and social security contributions the solution to Europe's political and economic problems find the East's penchant for liberalisation difficult to accept. Furthermore, rich countries – net contributors to the EU budget – may start to chafe at supporting poorer neighbours, which, in the eyes of their citizenry, 'steal' jobs through 'unfair' competition. For instance, in 2004 President Chirac of France criticised the ex-communist countries for undermining European unity by bringing in low corporate taxes and Chancellor Schröder of Germany pointedly remarked that they took aid from Brussels while stealing businesses from western Europe.

Yet whatever the problems for producers, it is undeniable that more competition brings huge benefits to EU customers in the form of cheaper goods and services. And EU-15 firms can enhance their competitiveness by redeployment of investment and labour. Of course, that may inflict (short-term) pain, chiefly on those who are made redundant as a result of relocation or outsourcing. But it is what renders countries more affluent: 'A policy locking people into jobs that could be better done elsewhere is self-defeating' (Economist, 2007a: 12). Integration – and, more generally, globalisation – highlights the need for a flexible, dynamic labour market and a well-educated, adaptable workforce (see below).

Thus enlargement provides a major opportunity to liberalise European economies. The entry of countries from central and eastern Europe can be metaphorically seen as an injection of fresh blood (see also Rennie, 2008: 3). By enhancing heterogeneity, spurring competition and undermining the old ways, the process of enlargement constitutes a powerful impulse to change and reform. This is of particular relevance in the context of the abortive attempts to implement the Lisbon Strategy (Munkhammar, 2007). Yet, for that to happen, politicians and technocrats have to convince Europeans (and themselves) that globalisation and market forces should be seen more as a chance for prosperity than a menace.

The condition of European business

In sharp contrast to the USA or Asia, continental Europe is often portrayed as a has-been whose potential is shackled by the hostile business climate resulting from excessive government interventionism. High income redistribution and generous welfare provisions, ubiquitous red tape and tightly regulated product markets, high non-wage labour costs and a heavy tax burden, stringent labour laws and militant trade unions dominating old industries are all seen as the root causes of Old Europe's unimpressive economic performance in recent years.

In 2001–06 the USA managed an average growth rate of 2.5 per cent a year. That of Europe (EU-15) was only 1.5 per cent. Over the same period, unemployment in the USA stood at 4–5 per cent; in the EU it was 9–10 per cent. The USA's advantages include a truly single market, a youthful population, higher labour productivity and first-rate universities (see below). Compared with the USA and Asia, the EU is regarded as less dynamic, entrepreneurial, innovation-oriented and less willing to embrace globalisation. Many European politicians, fearful of the rise of China and India as well as the dynamism and business friendliness of several eastern European countries, take the view that protectionism in its multifaceted forms is an appropriate way of defending national interests and local jobs. Blocking foreign takeovers, hindering EU-wide labour mobility, obstructing trade liberalisation and inveighing against production relocation to the east all exemplify this stance: Nicolas Sarkozy's 'anti-undiluted-competition' change to the EU constitution is a case in point here.

Yet the overall picture is ambiguous. EU business argues that, despite operating in a difficult political, social and economic environment, it has managed to retain 16 of the top 30 international companies by revenue. Indeed, the EU has around 30 per cent of the world's leading 2,000 companies, approximately in line with its 30 per cent share of world GDP (Carson, 2007: 4). EU companies not only successfully vie with US and Asian businesses, but also make equally high returns on equity as their US counterparts. Notwithstanding the hostile business climate, EU business has proved resilient in the face of competition from Asia. German small and medium-sized enterprises (*Mittelstand*), in particular, have succeeded in becoming world leaders in tiny niche markets.

That said, it is necessary to bear in mind a number of serious caveats. Above all, Europe excels only in 'old-economy' industries such as car-making or luxury goods; in high-tech sectors, it lags far behind the USA. The broadly defined ICT and bio-tech industries are dominated by US firms such as Google, Intel, Microsoft, IBM, Amgen and Genetech.[1] There are many reasons for that: the USA accounts for 40 per cent of total world spending on R&D and produces 63 per cent of the most frequently cited publications (National Defence Research Institute, 2008: 46–7). It is home to 30 of the world's 40 leading universities (Shanghai Jiao Tong University, 2008), and employs 70 per cent of the world's living Nobel laureates. Last but not least, the USA produces 38 per cent of patented new technologies in the OECD and employs 37 per cent of the researchers (National Defence Research Institute, 2008: 63). And, being particularly strong in downstream innovation and entrepreneurship, it successfully turns numerous scientific advances into profitable businesses. All of which might go

---

1   American firms annually spend approximately $200 billion on research and development. In 2006, for example, Microsoft spent $6.6 billion on research and development, IBM and Intel around $6 billion, and Cisco Systems and HP $4 billion each.

some way towards explaining why the innovation gap between the USA and the EU, albeit declining of late, is still considerable (PRO INNO Europe, 2008: 15).

Structural weaknesses of continental Europe

The USA's 'new-economy' dominance is intertwined with the structure of its economy. In modern developed economies (the USA, Japan and western Europe) it is the service sector, which encompasses a wide array of activities from low-tech plumbing to software writing or website design, which generates new jobs. In Anglo-Saxon economies services account for three-quarters of income and four-fifths of jobs. Yet in France, Germany and Italy the service sector accounts for six to ten percentage points fewer in terms of income and jobs. In continental Europe a relatively large proportion of the workforce is still employed in union-dominated manufacturing.

Services should not only be associated with low-skilled jobs in hotels and restaurants, but also with high-skilled occupations. Big retailers are now the world's most high-tech-intensive companies. Considering the stress laid in the Lisbon Strategy on the necessity to develop a knowledge-based economy, the size of the service sector might be regarded as an emblem of modernity. From this point of view, continental Europe can be regarded as less advanced than the USA (and other Anglo-Saxon countries, including the UK and Ireland). The flow of jobs and capital from declining to expanding industries in Germany, France and Italy has not been as high as in Britain or the USA (Zientara, 2006a: 49).

Why does continental Europe lag in this important respect

behind the USA and the Anglo-Saxon EU member states? What really lies behind this phenomenon is strict employment protection legislation (EPL) coupled with high union protection. Countries with stricter employment protection legislation and higher union protection have lower rates of employment in the service sector. They prevent the movement of labour from low-productivity to high-productivity occupations. In recent years, owing to globalisation-driven trade and the rapid pace of technological progress, the process of job churning has intensified. Businesses are set up and wound up on a larger scale than in the recent past. The acceleration of job churning is spurred by innovation. As new products – often intangible products – are devised, service-sector firms are established to bring them to the market. Furthermore, an increasing number of tangible goods are endowed with a 'knowledge input' in the form of design, technology or customer service (Woodall, 2000: 29). For example, the latest models of cars are so technologically advanced that no amateur mechanic can repair the simplest defect without recourse to a service station.

Thus stringent EPL, by imposing additional costs and constraints on existing and *potential* employers, acts as an impediment to the creation of more productive jobs and growth of the service sector in continental Europe. EPL also acts as a disincentive to existing employers to lay off labour (because the costs are higher) and to existing employees to change jobs (because they are protected in their existing environment). Yet the laying off of labour is a crucial part of the process of jobs moving from less productive to more productive sectors. In the same vein, excessive red tape, which complicates and lengthens the process of starting up businesses, stifles entrepreneurship and is not conducive to generating new employment. While deindustrialisation, or the disappearance of industrial jobs, is often regarded as a sign of economic decline, in a deregulated economy it can be a sign of renewal.

In continental Europe, a considerable proportion of the workforce still holds posts in the manufacturing sector, which is also dominated by trade unions. Unions in the manufacturing sector thwart efforts to ease EPL to protect their own jobs (Gelauff and Pomp, 2000). EPL has two opposite effects. It both prevents some existing employees becoming unemployed and makes it harder for job-seekers to get employment. This suggests that EPL may cause the emergence of an 'insider-outsider' labour market.

Insiders – people on permanent contracts in well-protected employment – see free-market reform as ending their privileged status as protected insiders (Zientara, 2008a). To them, the possible gains from change are worth less than the risk of losing what they already possess (Economist, 2006b: 32). As a result of the success of insiders in protecting their own status, outsiders – that is, job-seekers and those on temporary contracts – do not benefit from employment security and stand less chance of entering the inner circle. Thus, a two-tier system emerges. According to this analysis, the campaigns of trade unionists are entirely rational from a self-interested point of view.

This could provide a causal explanation of the statistical correlation between employment protection legislation, unionisation and slow growth in services: high protection of unionised jobs that are predominant in manufacturing[2] reinforces unions' power as insiders; unions use their clout to preserve labour

---

2   In the words of Paul Hofheinz: 'We [Europeans] tend to think of the economy as manufacturing, and of jobs in terms of industrial jobs, with a big salary, lots of benefits and security' (cited in Economist, 2006a: 28).

market rigidities which hold back the expansion of job-providing services; those outside employment lose as new service industries do not expand; those already inside the labour market gain from increased job security, at least in the short term.

Yet there is far more to it than that. Under union pressure, in Europe priority is given to current consumption – in the form of generous welfare provisions or public aid to agriculture and declining industries – rather than either private or government investment in education or R&D. In 2007 Europeans spent an average of $10,191 per student (measured at PPP) compared with $22,476 in the USA. They devoted only 1.3 per cent of GDP to higher education, compared with 2.9 per cent in the USA (Economist, 2008: 35). In the same year total expenditure on R&D amounted to 1.8 per cent of GDP in the EU and 2.6 per cent in the USA (PRO INNO Europe, 2008: 39). Likewise, in the EU public spending on ICT stood at 6.4 per cent of GDP, and in the USA at 6.7 per cent. Less money spent on education and R&D affects the capacity to innovate, which is seen as the key to preserving a competitive advantage in a knowledge-based economy (Porter, 1990; European Commission, 2007c: 7). There is a growing risk, therefore, that the entire EU – and continental economies in particular – will fall behind the USA and parts of Asia (PRO INNO Europe, 2008).

Equally importantly, spending on innovation and new technologies enhances productivity. Higher rates of investment in ICT in the USA and the UK have led to faster productivity growth in services. Since 1995, productivity growth in the service sector has been less than 0.5 per cent a year in the euro zone, 2 per cent in the UK and 3 per cent in the USA (Economist, 2006a: 28). This not only boosts service industries, but also translates into higher living standards.

Furthermore, the key to long-term development requires removal of the barriers that prevent labour and capital flowing from declining to prospective industries (Zientara, 2006a). As the industrial revolution gathered strength 200 years ago, labour moved from agriculture and low-scale production to manufacturing. This was possible because in the nineteenth century employment protection legislation and union protection were very low or non-existent. Today, with the shift to a knowledge-based economy, resources have to be transferred from (declining) manufacturing to expanding services. For this to happen, we need more flexibility – which implies less strict EPL, lower union protection, less generous welfare benefits and less regulation. In sum, notwithstanding the resilience and record profits of EU businesses, the biggest continental economies are still structurally weak.

Granted, progress has been made in liberalising financial markets, but this was the least controversial area, whose reform did not run counter to powerful vested interests. Likewise, markets for goods and, to a lesser extent, services were considerably freed. But liberalisation of labour markets – the most important and most difficult – has markedly failed to materialise.[3] Reluctant to press on with free-market reform, some politicians increasingly speak of pan-European harmonisation. That would

3 Such a sequence of reforms is typical. First, financial markets are liberalised, then markets for goods and services, and finally labour markets. In theory, financial liberalisation renders job-market reform easier; by reducing the cost of capital, it lowers consumer prices and hence increases real wages. Competitive markets for products also squeeze profit margins and drive consumer prices down, thereby pushing real wages up. Businesses will then attempt to reduce labour costs and to loosen fire-and-hire constraints. At that point, however, insiders (trade unions) – aware that their vital interests are threatened – intervene and frustrate liberalisation efforts.

entail harmonising labour laws, welfare benefits and tax rates so that central and eastern European countries could not use their comparative advantage of lower labour costs.

From the perspective of EU-12 countries, yielding to that pressure and backtracking on free-market reform would spell disaster. With far lower labour productivity, lower-quality infrastructure and very few world-class companies, accepting a Western-style welfare state together with restrictive fire-and-hire procedures might act as a disincentive to foreign investors and local entrepreneurs alike, and slow down economic growth and the catching-up process. The negative results of such a policy would fall disproportionately on the poor living mainly in depressed, retarded regions of the EU-12. Thus, as will become clear throughout this monograph, the key to the 'catching up' of the EU regions does not lie in a harmonisation of social benefits and employment protection legislation – that would prevent the very economic change that is necessary. Neither does it lie in an active regional policy involving redistribution. Rather the key lies with the removal of barriers to growth. The regional income and productivity differences in New Europe are very significant as a result of the economic legacy of communism. The EU-12 must be allowed, indeed encouraged, to liberalise their economies in order to help them catch up with the EU-15 and to allow the most backward regions to catch up with the most prosperous.

4 TWO ASPECTS OF EU REGIONAL POLICY

This chapter focuses on the implications of EU regionalism in general and the concept of a 'Europe of regions' in particular for the standing of national governments. We present – within the wider framework of cohesion policy – the instruments of regional policy, as well as the principles of national regional state aid, to show the magnitude and mechanisms of the support designed to help less prosperous regions.

Socio-political implications of EU regionalism

Some regard the EU as a mosaic of regions, which differ from one another – economically, politically, linguistically and culturally – to a larger degree than the member states themselves differ. This perspective has laid the foundations of an increasingly popular school of thought, known as the 'Europe of regions'. Seen in this way, the EU comes across not as an alliance of nation-states determined to follow the path of deeper integration, but as an overarching grouping of more or less self-governing regions. While accepting a common European identity, they cultivate their local distinctiveness and pursue their own development agenda. As Ederveen and Pelkmans (2006: 9) note, the principle of subsidiarity, which constitutes one of the fundamentals of the EU's rationale, should not be synonymously identified with lower-level decision-making; 'rather, it involves a careful assessment of the optimal level at which decisions should be taken'.[1]

This has profound ramifications for governance issues within the EU itself and for the increasingly complex relationship between the EU institutions, member states and regions themselves. It is sometimes argued that the Commission, while constantly referring to the significance of subsidiarity, somehow purposefully 'invents' regional problems so as to deal directly with the regions that are often conceived by EU bureaucrats.[2] That view is not completely baseless.

It is also argued in this context that the regional focus of cohesion policy is not appropriate (Sapir et al., 2004; Santos, 2008). 'Instead, it should be at the level of the Member State that the distributive element of cohesion policy operates, leaving Member States to determine their own priorities' (Begg, 2008: 7). This has particularly significant ramifications for the recently acceded countries of central and eastern Europe, which,

---

1   It has to be stressed that the principle of subsidiarity can also be interpreted as implying the dichotomy 'government' versus 'non-government'. Such an interpretation shifts the focus from the optimal level of institutional/governmental decision-making to the question of whether a given decision should be taken by any sort of government – be it central or regional – or by an individual himself. The principle of subsidiarity is not new and appears in Catholic Church doctrine – though the EU interpretation of it is far more state-centric than the Catholic Church interpretation.

2   Some argue that the intensification of globalisation processes leads to the decline of the state (Ohmae, 1995) and to the erosion of state territoriality (see Chapter 5). This is because the greater mobility of capital enfeebles – if not undermines – the state's capacity to regulate economic activity within its boundaries. As Brenner (1999) points out, 'this on-going re-scaling of territoriality is simultaneously transferring state power upwards to supranational agencies such as the European Union (EU) and devolving it down towards the state's regional and local levels, which are better positioned to promote and regulate urban-regional restructuring' (p. 439).

as we have seen, not only lag behind the old members, but also are marked by the biggest regional disparities. It follows that – if the focus of cohesion policy were to shift from the regional scale to the national one – central and eastern European policy-makers might decide to promote national development – by, for example, supporting economically strong regions acting as drivers of growth – disregarding territorial imbalances and core–periphery divides. This postulate, irrespective of its rationale and wider implications (see also Chapters 8 and 9), touches upon the question of decentralisation and power devolution.

Under communism, Poland and other Soviet-bloc members were highly centralised. Communism not only did away with market forces (Mises, 1949; Hayek, 1960), but also suppressed democracy at national and regional level (Balcerowicz, 2003). One-party rule stifled political dissent and frowned upon any grassroots activism; it also ruled out power devolution and regional self-government. It was apparatchiks – appointed by capital-city-headquartered, central politburo members – who headed urban and regional governing institutions.

Indeed, one of the most significant achievements of the reforms carried through after 1989 was to devolve *some* power to regions and to give local residents the right to elect directly city mayors, heads of local administrative units and municipal councillors. It is fair to claim that there has been a progressive revival of broadly understood regionalism in many central and eastern European countries. This manifests itself in various forms, visible in the sociocultural sphere and also in matters of politics. In many Polish regions after the November 2006 local elections, for example, the parties that were unable to build a consensus at national level succeeded in forming local ruling coalitions

(National Electoral Office, 2006). Local party leaders pointed out that certain ideological differences must be (pragmatically) brushed aside for the sake of the prosperity of *their* region.

Moreover, this newly born regionalism has moved – together with hundreds of thousands of Poles leaving their country in search of better prospects – beyond the Polish borders and taken on a new significance. As EU citizens, Poles working in the UK, Ireland and other European countries have the right to participate in local (but not national) elections. Considering the massive scale of the post-accession migration, they constitute a potentially influential electorate, whose voices might prove decisive in many local elections held in the EU-15. Before the 2007 elections, Scottish politicians were busy currying favour with thousands of Poles living in Scotland.

But there is more to the renaissance of local civic activism than meets the eye. That sense of civic belonging – which for years had been discouraged by communist authorities – is closely intertwined with such key notions as interaction, cooperation, trust, partnership and consensus-seeking, which increases the capacity of a community to achieve a common objective. This, in turn, bears upon a wider question – namely, the part social capital plays in regional development (Putnam, 1995; Pastor et al., 2000; Maskell, 2001; Trigilia, 2001; Tura and Harmaamkorpi, 2005), which, as we will see, is of great pertinence to Poland (see Chapters 7 and 10).

Although communism is a thing of the past, its control-and-command nature still has an alluring charm for many central and eastern European politicians. The emphasis placed by the EU on both subsidiarity and regional issues does not have to be a prelude, as some commentators imply, to increasing

Community-wide income redistribution. But if money transfers to depressed EU regions are combined with nationwide free-market reform, they may well help solve some regional problems.

The principles and instruments of EU cohesion policy

EU cohesion policy, governed by Articles 2 and 4, and Title XVII of the Treaty Establishing the European Community (TEC), aims to promote socio-economic convergence (Leonardi, 2005). Article 158 of the TEC stipulates that the Community 'shall aim at reducing disparities between the levels of development of the various regions and the backwardness of the least favoured regions or islands, including rural areas'. In practice, as has been noted, economic and social cohesion is defined in terms of reducing regional disparities as measured by GDP per head (relative to the EU average) in PPP terms. It follows that EU cohesion policy is de facto regional in character, although the Lisbon Treaty (assuming it is ever adopted) will slightly shift its focus from regional to 'territorial' (Begg, 2008: 3).

Given that enlargement contributed to widening socio-economic regional disparities, as the European Commission (2007b) pointed out, cohesion policy was redesigned in the context of an enlarged Union as well as in the context of the progress of globalisation and the increasing importance of a knowledge economy. Furthermore, the European Commission (ibid.) highlights that cohesion policy is not in conflict with the goals of the Lisbon Strategy of promoting growth and employment. The Community Strategic Guidelines also play up that link, listing three overarching priorities: (1) improving the attractiveness of regions; (2) encouraging innovation and entrepreneurship;

(3) fostering better jobs and developing human resources (European Council, 2006).

These assertions, however, are somehow problematic given that, for one thing, cohesion policy is regarded primarily as a distributive policy and, for another, growth requires resources to be concentrated on where they are most productive (Santos, 2008) (see also Chapter 9). In fact, what it comes down to is that, in the words of Begg (2008), 'cohesion policy is awkwardly positioned within two overlapping sets of tensions. The first is between distributive and allocative objectives, while the second is between the imperatives of the Lisbon strategy and the demands of convergence in economic activity' (p. 4).

The simplified framework of cohesion policy is based on three objectives – (1) convergence; (2) regional competitiveness and employment; (3) EU territorial cooperation. The three main sources of financing for these actions include the European Regional Development Fund (ERDF) and the European Social Fund (ESF) – the Structural Funds – and the Cohesion Fund.[3] The creation of a new cross-border cooperation structure was also proposed with a view to allowing members' regional and local authorities to cope with the traditional legal and administrative problems that come up when managing cross-border programmes and projects.

Member states with a gross national income (GNI) less than 90 per cent of the EU average are eligible for assistance through

3   The Cohesion Fund finances up to 85 per cent of the eligible expenditure of major projects involving the environment and transport infrastructure. This is supposed to strengthen cohesion and solidarity within the EU. Eligible are the least prosperous member states of the Union whose gross national product (GNP) per capita is below 90 per cent of the EU-25 average. So, in addition to the EU-12, in 2007 Greece, Portugal and Spain were also eligible.

the Cohesion Fund. More pertinently, regions with per capita GDP less than 75 per cent of the EU-25 average qualify for the ERDF and ESF support under the 'Convergence Objective' (former 'Objective 1'). What is more, temporary support is also made available to those regions where per capita GDP would have been below 75 per cent of the EU-15 average (the so-called statistical effect of enlargement). All remaining regions are eligible for support through the 'Competitiveness and Employment Objective' ('Objective 2'). Likewise, all regions are eligible for the 'Territorial Cooperation Objective' ('Objective 3').

The ERDF aims to reduce disparities between the levels of development of various regions and the backwardness of the least-favoured regions, including rural and peripheral areas. Its resources are mainly used to co-finance infrastructure, productive investment leading to the creation or maintenance of jobs, as well as local development initiatives and the business activities of small and medium-sized enterprises. The ESF, in turn, provides significant support to achieve progress towards full employment and to improve quality and productivity at work, as well as to promote social inclusion and cohesion. It promotes investment in human resources management, equal opportunities and boosts human potential/capital in the domain of R&D. The Cohesion Fund assists the eligible member states to catch up with Europe's better-off regions by contributing to the improvement of transport, energy and environmental infrastructure.[4]

As explained in European Commission (2007b), the priority has shifted to help fund programmes focusing on innovation,

4   As we will see, this emphasis on infrastructure is of great importance to Poland, whose development is hindered by, among other things, infrastructure in disrepair.

environmental protection, risk prevention, accessibility to transport and telecommunications infrastructure and investment in human capital. This is, as noted in the Introduction, in recognition of the role the cohesion policy can play in helping the EU reach the goals of the Lisbon Strategy of higher growth and employment.

Still, the fundamental role of cohesion policy is to ensure that regions lagging behind the European average in terms of development are offered the means to catch up via investment in infrastructure and human resources. As well as the added value to the member states that comes through the exchange of experience, expertise and best practice, the funds also promote good governance and provide secure funding over a seven-year period. In the programming period 2007–13, some €35 billion per year will be spent on the various Structural Funds, while the amount spent on the Cohesion Fund will grow from €7 billion to €10 billion in 2013 (European Commission, 2007a).

But all this should not be accepted without question, not least because much more needs to be done (in the area of internal structural change in the EU) so as to make best possible use of the European taxpayer's money.

The rationale of national regional state aid

In addition to the EU Structural Funds and the Cohesion Fund, individual countries provide regional state aid. This is often addressed to large companies that carry out economic activity or intend to set up in selected disadvantaged areas. The idea is again to redress regional disparities and ensure socio-economic development in poor regions by supporting investment and job creation

Table 6 Share (%) of the population that lives in regions eligible for national regional aid in 2007–13

Member state	Regions with a per capita GDP lower than 75% of the Community average	Regions with a per capita GDP higher than 75% of the Community average owing to the statistical effect	'Economic development' regions and low-density regions
Austria	0.0	3.4	0.0
Belgium	0.0	12.4	0.0
Denmark	0.0	0.0	0.0
Finland	0.0	0.0	23.7
France	2.9	0.0	0.0
Germany	12.5	6.1	0.0
Greece	36.6	55.5	7.9
Ireland	0.0	0.0	26.5
Italy	29.2	1.0	2.9
Luxembourg	0.0	0.0	0.0
Netherlands	0.0	0.0	0.0
Portugal	70.1	3.8	0.0
Sweden	0.0	0.0	13.0
Spain	36.2	5.8	16.6
UK	4.0	0.6	4.4
EU-15	15.0	4.3	4.0
Cyprus	0.0	0.0	0.0

Member state	Regions with a per capita GDP lower than 75% of the Community average	Regions with a per capita GDP higher than 75% of the Community average owing to the statistical effect	'Economic development' regions and low-density regions
Czech Republic	88.6	0.0	0.0
Estonia	100.0	0.0	0.0
Hungary	72.2	0.0	0.0
Latvia	100.0	0.0	0.0
Lithuania	100.0	0.0	0.0
Malta	100.0	0.0	0.0
Poland	100.0	0.0	0.0
Slovakia	88.9	0.0	0.0
Slovenia	100.0	0.0	0.0
EU-25	27.7	3.6	4.0
Bulgaria	100.0	0.0	0.0
Romania	100.0	0.0	0.0
EU-27	32.2	3.4	3.7

Sources: European Commission (2006), Communication from Mrs Kroes to the Commission: Guidelines on National Regional State Aid for 2007–2013, Brussels; A. A. Ambroziak (2006), 'Criteria for granting national regional state aid in 2007–2013', Wspólnoty Europejskie, 2, Warsaw: Foreign Trade Research Institute, p. 13

(European Commission, 2006: 13). Specifically, it is directed to companies that decide to: (1) establish a new business in economically weak regions; (2) expand an existing company; (3) diversify production so as to launch a completely new product; (4) change the production process; or (5) take over a company that has just been shut down or risks being wound up (if no buyer is found).

The Commission (ibid.) takes the view that national regional aid – which is supposed to promote the economic, social and territorial cohesion of the EU as a whole – may be considered, on the basis of Article 87 (3) (a) and (c) of the EC Treaty, to be compatible with the common market (p. 13). In other words, the Commission deems national assistance potentially effective and hence justified on competition grounds. It explicitly states, however, that – while designed to assist the development of the most disadvantaged regions – national regional assistance should be used *sparingly* and *proportionately*.

The criteria applied by the Commission when examining the compatibility of national regional aid with the principles of the common market were codified in the 1998 guidelines on national regional aid, which cover the period 2000–06 (European Commission, 1998). They were subsequently modified to allow for the consequences of enlargement. Hence the 2007–13 guidelines fix the limit for the overall population coverage of 42 per cent of the Community of 25 member states, which was expected to rise to 45.5 per cent following the accession of Romania and Bulgaria (European Commission, 2006: 15). Likewise, the Commission considers that the conditions are fulfilled if a region has a per capita GDP (at PPP) of less than 75 per cent of the Community average (27.7 per cent of the EU-25 population lived in such regions in 2006).

In addition, other regions that theoretically do not meet the above eligibility criteria are allowed – owing to specific circumstances – to benefit from national regional aid. These include among others: (1) those regions whose GDP per capita exceeds 75 per cent of the Community average solely because of the statistical effect of enlargement; (2) so-called 'economic development' regions; (3) low-density regions.[5] Table 6 presents the share of the population of EU countries that lives in regions eligible for national regional aid in 2007–13.[6]

To summarise, poorer regions can benefit both from EU regional aid (that is, the Structural Funds and the Cohesion Fund) as well as national regional state aid. Nearly all of New Europe's population live in regions that are eligible for the two kinds of assistance. Whereas the rationale of EU regional subsidies may be justifiable, the *raison d'être* of national state aid is open to doubt; the Commission itself stresses that it should be used sparingly and under exceptional circumstances.

Indeed – in view of the Commission's (2007b) recognition of the implications of a knowledge-based economy as well as the aforesaid (putative) relaunch of the Lisbon Strategy – one can discern the tendency to shift the emphasis from the traditional welfare transfers of a permanent character[7] and sector-oriented subsidies to help targeted on concrete projects aiming to encourage innovation generation as well as to improve (ICT) infrastructure and human capital (computer skills).

---

5 For the full list of eligible regions, see European Commission (2006: 18–19).

6 Note that the table includes only the main categories of eligible regions.

7 For instance, so-called (EU-funded) structural pensions for Polish farmers who decide to give up work and hand their farms to their children.

5 THE CHALLENGES OF GLOBALISATION

This chapter, while referring to the basic classification of Europe's regions and urban areas, analyses the general character of challenges posed by the globalisation and integration processes. Particular attention is paid to the question of whether globalisation might indeed be undermining urban and regional democracy.

European regions and the challenges of globalisation

The acceleration of globalisation, the shift to a knowledge-based economy and the propagation of ICT have dramatically affected the regional agenda. These phenomena coincided with the resurgence of interest in the region as a scale of economic organisation (Scott, 1996, 1998; Storper, 1997; Armstrong and Taylor, 2000).

As the OECD (2006: 26) points out, 'globalisation and the shift to services-based (particularly knowledge-based) economies increasingly challenge countries to make the best of their regional assets. In this process, sub-national areas are competing across national boundaries'. Whereas the European Commission (2006: 13) places special emphasis on the necessity to redress regional disparities, the OECD adopts a slightly different approach to regional issues. It unambiguously states that 'regional development policies are no longer considered a tool to reduce socio-economic disparities across national territory, but an active strategy to foster regional innovation, and to turn place-based competitive advantages into drivers of national economic growth' (OECD, 2006: 26). In this sense, it is essential to stress the contrast between the EU's preoccupation with reducing regional disparities and the OECD's concern with promoting economic growth.

Globalisation, while increasing competition, offers areas new investment and trade opportunities. Indeed, regional differences remain the principal source of regions' comparative advantage. As such, globalisation can emphasise local characteristics but, at the same time, allowing local areas to capitalise on foreign direct investment (FDI) and international commerce, which, in turn, translates into higher rates of economic growth and prosperity (see also Krugman and Venables, 1995). In sum, the two scales – in line with the main tenet of liberalism – are not incompatible with each other and result in 'win-win' outcomes.

The critics of globalisation

Yet a growing number of critics highlight the negative conse-quences of globalisation (see, *inter alia*, Leitner and Shepard, 1997; Keil, 2000; Goodhart, 2001; Davis, 1998; Featherstone, 2003; DeFilipis, 2004; Purcell, 2006). It is argued that globalisa-tion, on the one hand, intensifies the process of deterritorialisa-tion (Appadurai, 1996) and, on the other, prompts restructuring and 'creative destruction' of politico-economic spaces at various geographical scales. It is assumed that capital intrinsically seeks to do away with assorted obstacles to its circulation – an objective that can be attained mainly through 'the construction of relatively fixed and immobile transport, communications and regulatory-institutional infrastructures' (Brenner, 1999: 433). In consequence, as Jensen and Richardson (2004) point out, one can discern a perceived drive to create a single economically frictionless European space, with a transportation infrastructure designed and built according to the apparent need for global competitiveness.

It is further argued that, owing to the ever more intense necessity to attract foreign direct investment, the decision-making process at local level risks being 'hijacked' by forces that are global in character and hence unaccountable to the local public (Holston, 1999; Goodhart, 2001; DeFilipis, 2004; Purcell, 2006). Of course, given the vital role cities play in today's increasingly globalised reality (Sassen, 1993), it is urban areas which find themselves particularly exposed to the local–global interaction. It follows that decisions that determine the urban environment are perceived to be taken with a view to serving the interests of shareholders rather than those of citizens. In other words, it is argued that: 'urban governing institutions … are becoming less a democratic forum for citizens to make decisions and more a tool to ensure that the area competes effectively for capital investment … Thus institutions like public–private partnerships, appointed competitiveness councils and quasi-public agencies are increasingly making decisions that were formerly made by elected officials directly accountable to the public' (Purcell, 2006: 1922–3).

Furthermore, globalisation allows firms to restructure and cut costs on a far bigger scale than in the past. They increasingly shift production or outsource business functions to lower-cost countries, which leads to redundancies and plant closures.

This, coupled with the scale-down of state-financed welfare programmes and the stress on deregulation and privatisation, it is argued, increases the sense of insecurity and prompts the growth in material inequality (Gill, 1996). Drawing on the experience of Los Angeles, Davis (1998) points out that, while the high-wage service sector expands, well-paid manufacturing jobs are transferred elsewhere and replaced by lower-paying service jobs. On the whole, they assume that globalisation reduces welfare and fosters inequality (see also MacLeod, 2002).[1] For these reasons, it is even suggested that the principal political division line at urban/local level runs between those who favour democracy, social justice and environmental sustainability and those who advocate the necessity of free-market-based solutions (Keil, 2000: 760).

The complex reality of the impact of globalisation

There is little doubt that globalisation is a long-term and uneven process. But the analysis of the critics of globalisation and its impact on governmental autonomy is too simplistic. Some professional groups and regions suffer disproportionately in the short term (see also Economist, 2007a). This might justify temporary assistance to such groups in the form of requalification schemes. Of course, central and eastern Europe have benefited from international capital flows – but not all regions have done so. It is large metropolitan areas and core regions which seem to have benefited

---

1   Tellingly, several well-known American economists, including Paul Krugman, the 2008 Nobel Prize laureate, and Larry Summers, a former Treasury secretary, have begun to doubt whether globalisation is really beneficial to Americans. They also suggest that, rather than improving living standards, 'global integration may be causing wage stagnation, widening inequality and greater insecurity' (Beddoes, 2008: 32–3).

Box 1 Classification and hierarchy of EU urban centres

All European cities fall into one of the three basic categories, defined on the basis of population size: (1) large cities (with populations over 250,000); (2) medium-sized cities with populations between 100,000 and 250,000; and (3) small cities with populations not exceeding 100,000. But even the European average varies across member states. For example, nineteen French cities have a population of over 250,000 (2001) each, but Clermont-Ferrand (261,000 inhabitants) and Nancy (258,000) are regarded as second-tier cities. In contrast, Portugal has only six cities with populations of over 100,000. Owing to their role of provincial capitals, smaller cities such as Aveiro (73,000) are identified as medium-sized. Twelve Polish cities have populations of over 250,000. Cities in new accession countries are generally not as populous as their Western counterparts.

What is more, a system has been developed based on the analysis in the European Spatial Development Perspective (ESDP) with a view to capturing the geographical relationship within the European urban hierarchy:

1 **Central High-Level Service Cities**: the largest cities (national capitals) and major commercial cities situated in the so-called 'Pentagon': London, Paris, Milan, Munich, Frankfurt, Hamburg, Amsterdam, Brussels and Luxembourg. They are all endowed with the highest multi-modal transport accessibility within the EU-27.

2 **Gateway Cities** (Sub-Continental Capitals): national capitals and major commercial cities outside the 'Pentagon' which act as first-rate service centres for

major parts of Europe: Madrid, Barcelona, Rome, Athens, Vienna, Berlin, Copenhagen, Prague, Warsaw, Budapest, Manchester, Lyon, Stuttgart and Leipzig.

3 **Smaller Capitals and Provincial Capitals**: smaller-scale equivalents of Gateway Cities: Dublin, Edinburgh, Lisbon, Helsinki, Stockholm, Bratislava, Ljubljana, Sofia, Bristol, Bordeaux, Strasbourg, Hanover, Poznań, Wrocław and Kraków.

4 **County Towns**: rural administrative and service centres for a surrounding area of 40–60 kilometres in radius, of which hundreds exist in Europe.

Source: OECD (2006: 27–8)

the most (see Box 1). Other smaller and traditional industry-dominated city regions together with peripheral (often rural) areas both in the EU-15 and the EU-12 are at a disadvantage and may struggle to benefit from the globalisation process.

Large metropolitan areas and economically strong city regions are characterised by advantages such as: (i) high-skilled HR (a highly qualified, educated workforce); (ii) well-developed infrastructure (roads, railways, airports, access to the Internet); (iii) availability of capital; (iv) higher-than-average market potential (considerable local purchasing power); (v) concentration of businesses (inter-firm linkages); and (vi) comparatively high quality of life[2] (see also Krugman, 1990; Sassen, 1993). Labour productivity

---

2   Given traffic congestion and higher crime rates, some may consider the quality of life there low, whereas others might value social and cultural amenities that smaller (provincial) towns and the countryside do not offer.

is also rather high in metropolitan areas and this can offset a relatively high cost of labour.[3]

Indeed, it could be argued that businesses establishing themselves in big cities and strong regions boost local economic activity, thereby further stimulating development arising from economies of agglomerations. That leads the greatest potential for growth to be in the regions already characterised by the greatest degree of economic activity (Krugman, 1995). It is also argued that large metropolitan areas act as contexts for innovation generation, thereby becoming engines of growth and sources of wealth (see also Sassen, 1993; Scott, 1996; Castells, 2001).

By contrast, other medium-sized city regions,[4] often situated in more peripheral areas, can be seen as less attractive owing to a

3   In this context, it is necessary to refer to geographical economics. One of its key findings is that free markets may not lead to economic equality across regions when firms can benefit from economies of scale. Krugman argues that firms might cluster near to a large market, leaving behind sparsely populated areas so as to make the most of scale economies and reduce the cost of transporting goods to their customers. Accordingly, as Brakman and Garretsen (2005) claim, thanks to increasing returns to scale, there has been a tendency towards increased concentration and agglomeration of economic activity in Europe (see also Janelle, 1969). Furthermore, due to the centripetal forces that continue to pull economic activity towards established centres, these areas can preserve tax rates that are higher than those in peripheral regions. This finding can both go some way towards explaining why increased economic integration within the EU has not led to a race to the bottom in socio-economic policy and, crucially, substantiate claims for more income redistribution (*de facto* from affluent regions to remote disadvantaged areas). However insightful these conclusions might appear, it is hard to accept the policy implication. Drawing on the experience of East German regions, we will make a case against pouring money into depressed areas while shunning economic reform (see Chapter 9).

4   A medium-sized city region (both in the EU-15 and the EU-12) is defined around one major medium-sized urban centre or possibly a number of smaller medium-sized cities. The medium-sized urban centres are in most cases regional or provincial capitals (see also Box 1).

less diversified skill base, lower productivity levels, less developed infrastructure (often in disrepair), and the obsolete structure of local economies. This applies in particular to those medium-sized regions whose local economic base was dominated by traditional industry (coal mining, steel making, low-end manufacturing) both in the EU-15 (North-East, Limburg in Belgium) and the EU-12 (Śląskie in Poland, Morawskoslezko in the Czech Republic, Nord-Est in Romania).[5]

In the past the competitive advantage of these old industrial regions, which came into being in the heyday of the Industrial Revolution, often derived from geographical proximity to raw materials (coal, iron ore). Yet, with deindustrialisation, this advantage has been lost.

For American or western European companies operating within national boundaries, the difference between the cost of labour in a big city and in a remote area might be significant. But for the same companies looking to invest in central and eastern Europe, wage differentials between large urban areas and peripheral regions are not sufficiently great to tempt companies to locate in the more distant regions. There is a big difference between the cost of labour in western and in central and eastern Europe: a Polish worker living in a big city costs 60–70 per cent less than his German counterpart. A Polish worker in a well-developed urban region, however, will cost only slightly more than a Polish worker in a peripheral region, with much less suitable human capital. It should be remembered that wage levels are always underpinned

5   Nonetheless, by offering a lower-cost skilled labour force, old industrial regions in eastern Europe have a relative edge over their western counterparts. This constitutes a short-term threat to traditional areas in the EU-15, which need to develop alternative sources of growth by drawing on the pool of existing experience, skill and knowledge (OECD, 2006: 32).

by social security benefits. This has the effect of reinforcing regional differentials.

This trend might be strengthened, if, as Graham and Marvin (2001) suggest, ICT networks polarise places and societies. As big urban areas enter the global network, they increasingly downplay the links with their surrounding regions. 'Glocal nodes' within large regions and cities link up with similar areas around the world, at the same time being increasingly loosely integrated with less developed neighbouring places. Residents of metropolitan areas all over the world tend to be better educated, share similar interests and, above all, speak English, which facilitates the polarisation of local communities. In EU-12 countries regional disparities in terms of education and ICT infrastructure are more conspicuous than in the EU-15,[6] so the consequences of these 'polarisation-inducing' processes might be even more dramatic. Central and eastern Europe's metropolitan areas have become increasingly cosmopolitan and internationalised. This presupposition is also borne out by the voting patterns in national and local elections: big cities across central and eastern Europe generally tend to vote for open-minded, economically liberal, technology-savvy politicians; the underdeveloped periphery tends to vote for traditionalists who often look at the Internet and the outside world with overt suspicion.

Graham and Marvin's (2001) insights might have far-reaching economic implications. What is at issue here is the emergence of a complex, non-linear relationship between ICT networks,

6   The residents of provincial towns and peripheral regions in central and eastern Europe are less likely to speak English and to be IT literate, compared with the situation in the West.

knowledge sharing and economic growth. Given that the development of ICT somehow plays down the importance of proximity, innovation generation might increasingly be transferred into and carried out in the global network, benefiting in the first place interconnected large metropolises, with the less developed periphery being progressively marginalised. So knowledge generated in this way, rather than spilling over to less technologically advanced surrounding areas, might enter the global network – which may be a network of prosperous urban regions – and thence be transferred or 'spirited away' elsewhere (see also Castells, 2001).

This, in turn, would be likely to enhance the already privileged standing of large urban areas, at the same time reinforcing the tendency towards a 'lopsided' distribution of technological advancement and economic growth. It follows that capital cities and well-developed regions in central and eastern Europe are, in all likelihood, on course to catch up with the EU average in the near future. But already depressed areas in the EU-12 periphery (and in the EU-15 for that matter) might develop at a far slower pace or be marginalised. This could cause regional disparities at European level to persist or even to widen. There is therefore a need to ensure that poorer regions can make best use of their comparative advantages and prevent these disparities from growing.

There have been concerns that the process of globalisation undermines local democracy and therefore centralises political decision-making. As it happens, there have been reforms to devolve power to Polish cities and regions and establish local and municipal self-government. This was largely a response to almost half a century of communist rule, when all decisions shaping the city and the region were taken by centrally and undemocratically appointed Communist Party members. In the eyes of those seeking devolution, a democracy functioning only at national level would not be tantamount to a genuine democracy. With little experience to draw on and the economy teetering on the brink of collapse in 1989/90 (Balcerowicz et al., 1997), the reformers were naturally inclined to see localised decision-making as more democratic and hence 'more desirable'. What they all had in mind was, above all, a conviction that in a truly democratic society people living in cities and regions have the right to govern themselves and to make decisions that shape their local environment (see also Chapter 7).

The biggest cities in Poland and elsewhere in central and eastern Europe are booming, being successful in attracting and keeping FDI. In the local elections held in Poland in November 2006, the residents of the metropolitan areas voted for those candidates who came out in favour of attracting international investors and encouraging local entrepreneurship, rather than those who wanted to increase public expenditure on social services and welfare benefits (National Electoral Office, 2006). Also, the inhabitants of the largest cities tend to see threats coming not from outside (from globalisation, multinationals, etc.), but from inside (cronyism, dishonesty and managerial incompetence on the part of municipal officials).

Big-city dwellers realise that without the inflow of international capital, the process of reducing the gap between the West and the East might be considerably slowed down (Zientara, 2008b). If the inhabitants of Poland's metropolitan areas elect pro-business, globalisation-friendly officials – thereby empowering them to pursue concrete development policy (which, among much else, consists in attracting foreign capital and managing EU funds) – so much the better. That is democracy at work. But there is more to this than meets the eye. ICT is a powerful vehicle for developing grassroots activism and reinforcing pluralism.[7] In fact, new technologies lend themselves particularly well to promoting democracy and citizenship awareness. In Poland local Internet forums, especially in the biggest cities, function as a platform for voicing one's discontent with municipal officials or discussing ways to sort out concrete problems such as traffic jams or infrastructure planning.

In this way, ICT, commonly associated with the global scale, also supports localisation and the more effective accountability of local government officials and representatives. Thus globalisation does not have to be seen as undermining urban democracy. This has wider implications for democracy in provincial towns and

7   This, in turn, is connected with another distinct – yet related – issue, namely the impact of ICT on regional development in general and the fortunes of disadvantaged, remote areas in particular. Much hope was pinned on the transformative effect of ICT (e-working, outsourcing). The OECD (2001b) came up with the endogenous-exogenous development approach (p. 32). The former implies that businesses in peripheral regions can make use of ICT to gain access to markets located in core areas, the latter that businesses in rich regions can, via ICT, take advantage of assets (mainly labour) in less favoured areas (Cornford et al., 1996; Castro and Jensen-Butler, 2003). It is increasingly clear, however, that some of the supposed benefits of ICT have failed to materialise (cf. Jæger and Storgaard, 1997; Clark, 2001; Schmied, 2002). A few studies demonstrate, for example, that e-working is a phenomenon typical of large cities rather than remote areas, where there are high commuting costs (Clark, 2001). As Gillespie et al. (2001) observe, for routine knowledge-based activities, there is a cost-driven tendency to their dispersal from high-cost metropolitan districts to lower-cost metropolitan areas – that is, from urban centres to suburbs and not from cities to remote regions (p. 22). And, with EU integration gathering momentum, office functions and business tasks that can be performed by means of ICT (call centres, say), rather than being outsourced to the West's periphery, are being contracted out to central and eastern European cities or even farther afield (see also Richardson and Belt, 2001).

technologically retarded peripheral areas. If they continue to lag behind big cities in terms of computer literacy and ICT infrastructure, not only might polarisation gather momentum, but local democracy might also be less effective.

All of this suggests that globalisation – rather than driving political changes and socio-economic development processes on the ground – is actually the result of various multifaceted interactions taking place at different geographical scales (McGuirk, 1997; Torrance, 2008; cf. Park, 2003; Cox, 2005). Indeed, McGuirk (1997) points out that it is erroneous 'to regard localities and regions as being at the mercy of external uncontrollable and mythologized global forces, because they are themselves a formative part of global processes' (p. 493). It follows that, rather than resisting 'external' forces, localities – to repeat – should try and capitalise on trade and investment opportunities (Kanter, 1995; Rusk, 1999) by, among other things, ensuring a favourable business climate (Dreier et al., 2001: 135). This implies that we should not agree with those researchers (Davis, 1998; Falk, 2000; MacLeod, 2002; Featherstone, 2003; Purcell, 2006) who call upon citizens to 'resist' neoliberal globalisation.

6 THE LEARNING REGION AND SOCIAL CAPITAL

In this chapter we discuss the ideas associated with the new regionalism, placing special emphasis on the concept of the 'learning region' and the significance of social capital. Having presented the critique of the new regionalism, we examine its relevance to the EU-12.

Innovation, learning and regional development

Nowadays knowledge in general and technological progress in particular are seen as principal determinants of growth (Porter, 1990; Barro and Sala-I-Martin, 1995). In practice, the rate of technological change and economic growth depends both on governments and firms. It is both politicians and managers who decide on how much to invest in research and development (R&D) and education (see Kealey, 1996). This highlights the significance of human capital. As economies are increasingly based on information processing and knowledge creation (Nonaka and Takeuchi, 1995), they require well-educated, highly skilled labour. There is evidence that countries investing in human capital and education grow faster than those spending less (Barro and Sala-I-Martin, 1995), while the presence of high-quality human capital has a positive effect on innovation generation (Armstrong and Taylor, 2000).[1]

There are two basic prerequisites of successful innovation:[2] information and the capacity to process and interpret it. Information has no meaning until it is complemented by personal knowledge and experience: i.e. until it is interpreted by a skilled person (Te Velde, 1999). It is also argued that innovation is inextricably entwined with employee creativity (Utterback, 1994; Amabile et al., 1996). Scott and Bruce (1994) point out that 'creativity has to do with the production of novel and useful ideas [...] and innovation has to do with the production and adaptation of useful ideas and idea implementation' (p. 581). In fact, organisational creativity in an R&D milieu is a subset of the broad domain of innovation (Chen and Kaufman, 2008).

Yet, critically, innovation processes have undergone a transformation from a basically linear process, whereby investment in R&D was supposed to produce inventions and innovation in relatively predictable contexts, into a non-linear, context-driven phenomenon (see, for instance, Kline and Rosenberg, 1986; Nonaka et al., 2000; Nonaka and Toyama, 2002; European Commission, 2007c; Peltokorpi et al., 2007). Thus innovation, underpinned by tacit-knowledge (Polanyi, 1966) transmission, is generated through interaction and cooperation that is specific to

---

1 Though it should not be assumed that government spending on these things generates growth – it can simply crowd out more efficient private spending.

2 Innovation should be distinguished from innovativeness. While the former takes the form of technological, product and process (TPP) innovations, the latter refers either to the importance of innovation (García and Calantone, 2001) or to an organisation's capacity to innovate (Hurley et al., 2005). 'Innovativeness relates to a series of individual and group level properties that are characteristics of group idea generation, learning, creativity and change. In this vein, innovativeness reflects the *potential* of organisations to produce innovative products [...]' (Paleo and Wijnberg, 2008: 4).

particular contexts (see also Castro and Jensen-Butler, 1991). That, in turn, accentuates the significance of (geographical) proximity (Fritsch and Schwirten, 1999) and the importance of institutions and social capital.

This is because, for one thing, distance hinders the exchange of tacit knowledge (Jaffe, 1989) and, for another, institutions and social capital facilitate cooperation. 'Proximity may thus economise on communication and interpretation costs involved in the creation of new knowledge' (Dolfsma, 2008: 69). This partially explains the resurgence of interest in the region, rather than the country, as a scale of economic organisation. In other words, it is the region which, by ensuring proximity and fostering local identity-based social bonds, seems to provide an environment particularly supportive of the above processes.[3] All of this led to the formulation of theories and doctrines that are associated with the new regionalism.[4]

The old regionalism focused on the support of inefficient industries, where there was no comparative advantage. The new regional economics focuses on encouraging local-scale cooperation between all regional actors and attempts to promote learning

3   Florida (2004) – who propagated the concept of the creative class whose 'members engage in work whose function is to "create meaningful new forms"' (p. 68) – argues that regions, in order to enhance their competitiveness, need to attract and retain creative people.

4   Generally speaking, the new regionalism is associated with a wide array of discourses and conceptualisations that came into prominence in the 1990s and differ considerably from the main tenets of the old regionalism (which itself refers to a body of theory and practice dominant in regional thinking approximately from the 1880s to the 1980s). It is possible to present in a simplified way the principal differences between the old and new regionalism in terms of notional dichotomies. Hence, while the old regionalism laid stress on government, coordination, formalism and closeness, the new regionalism emphasises the importance of governance, cooperation, trust and openness.

as well as to provide benign support to innovation-generating, technologically advanced industries, where there is a comparative advantage. This also applies to government-led initiatives aiming at forming clusters (European Commission, 2007c: 20). After all, the origins of Silicon Valley – the world's most renowned cluster (see also Saxenian, 1994) – could be traced back to the high levels of central government investment in defence during the cold war. Of course, the very conceptualisation of the cluster is deeply rooted in Marshall's (1890) industrial district argument (according to which there are three main factors – labour market, agglomeration externalities and knowledge infrastructure – that lie behind firms' location decisions).

There is, though, in the words of Michael Porter (2007), 'still confusion about policy implications. Should clusters be allowed to form spontaneously, which is what has usually occurred, or should there be some sort of policy intervention' (p. 20). In a letter to *The Economist*, Porter points out that

Cluster-policy thinking is very different from 'industrial policy' thinking, though many economists lump the two together. Cluster theory is neutral, rather than about picking winners, intervention, protection and subsidies. Clusters are good in any field because they boost productivity and innovation, and cluster policy seeks to reduce constraints and encourage externalities to raise the productivity of competition … There are literally hundreds of cluster initiatives all over the world today that are pursuing varying approaches to public–private collaboration to improve the business environment … While some of these initiatives will have limited impact, and a few may do harm … there are strong reasons to believe the cluster/region level will be a growing focus of economic policy. (Ibid.: 20–21)

Thus it is assumed that innovation generation proceeds most efficiently either in specialised clusters (Breschi and Malerba, 2005), where intra-firm links play a part (see also Wolfe and Gertler, 2004; Feldman et al., 2005), or in areas where industry, academia and other regional actors collaborate with each other to produce innovative solutions that trickle down to other entities or regions via the mechanism of knowledge spillovers (Jaffe, 1989).[5] Revilla Diez and Kiese (2006) point out that 'the extent to which a region succeeds in generating a continuous stream of TPP [technological, product and process] innovations depends primarily on its endowment with innovation actors (agents), and especially with innovating manufacturing firms, knowledge-intensive business services (KIBS) as well as research institutions' (p. 1006).

Furthermore, Malizia and Faser (1999) argue that the concentration of several companies in the same area is likely to give rise to positive externalities,[6] while Etzkowitz (2001) makes a case for the 'triple helix', which advocates localised synergies within the university–business–government triad. Anselin et al. (1997) confirm a positive link between university research and innovative activity. So the proximity of a university acts as an incentive for firms to locate near by in order to gain access to highly skilled

5   European Commission (2007c) points out that 'the traditional linear model of innovation […] is no longer relevant. […] Clusters may embody the characteristics of the modern innovation process' (p. 7).

6   The Marshall–Arrow–Romer (1890; 1962; 1986) concept of spillover externality, accentuating the role of specialisation, takes as its premise that industries cluster geographically to absorb knowledge spilling over between businesses. Regionally specialised industries grow faster because neighbouring firms learn from each other more effectively than geographically isolated firms. In contrast, Jacobs (1969) sees heterogeneity and diversification – not specialisation – as the essential factor behind concentration and, ultimately, regional growth. The externality in question stems from the cross-fertilisation of ideas between highly diversified businesses.

labour and to benefit from innovation (Lund, 1986; Jaffe, 1989). In a similar vein, Storper (1997) notes that, although academic R&D functions outside industry, innovation initially diffuses through personal contacts and interactions. It follows, to quote Dolfsma (2008: 69), that 'agglomerations not only offer the advantages of Marshall's "traded linkages", but possibly also the more elusive "untraded interdependencies" (Storper, 1997)'.

Of course, these ideas on their own do not make a case either for or against government intervention. Privately run and financed educational institutions may have better incentives than government-run and -financed institutions to participate in the process of creating a 'learning region' benefiting from externalities arising from innovation. Similarly, the development of industrial agglomerations with demand for an educated workforce may be a sufficient incentive for universities to orientate their education and research towards the needs of local industry. Whether government should be involved in this process is a separate matter from that of simply identifying that clusters and agglomerations are beneficial.

The concept of the learning region

This interplay between innovativeness, networking and proximity, in turn, lies at the core of the concept of the learning region, which some analysts regard as a breakthrough or a 'revolution in thinking' in regional policy (Armstrong and Taylor, 2000: 292). It shifts the focus from technological progress to wider socioeconomic change, highlighting that institutional and cultural factors are instrumental in ensuring such a transformation. Still, the learning region is an ambiguous concept with various nuances and connotations ascribed to it (see, for instance, Asheim, 1996; Morgan, 1997; Simmie, 1997; OECD, 2001a; Boekema et al., 2000).

In the event, Morgan (1997) sees it as the new generation of regional policy which, unlike traditional regional policy, accentuates the need to concentrate efforts on 'infostructure' (instead of infrastructure), integrated solving of local problems, permanent organisational learning and development of an information society. According to the OECD (2001a: 24), the learning region is characterised by 'regional institutions, which facilitate individual and organisational learning through the coordination of flexible networks of economic and political agents'. In consequence, the capacity of a region to create an environment supportive of processes of learning and innovation is seen as critical to preserving its competitive advantage.

Above all, it is accepted that modern economic systems are increasingly turning themselves into knowledge-driven economies. Hence, to follow the line of argument of Lundvall and Johnson (1994), if knowledge is the most important resource – and a driving force behind economic growth and societal advancement – learning is the most important process. Learning, therefore, is not viewed as an absorption of fixed and particular scientific knowledge, but as the process of (continual) change in institutional and organisational forms and economic structures. That is why socio-economic systems that are able to transform their structures in reaction to changed circumstances could best be described as learning economies.[7]

Furthermore, it is accepted that learning is, in essence, a

---

7   It should be noted that for Lundvall and Johnson (1994), the learning economy is a 'mixed economy' (p. 41), with the conspicuous presence of the public sector.

collective and interactive process.[8] And the regional level – rather than larger population units – may well be a very important level at which this takes place. So the regional scale is critical to turning 'old' economies into learning ones. Although regions affected by industrial decline are – as a rule – hard to reinvent (Cooke, 1995), this task is not impossible if there exists an environment that is adaptive to change. This will make it possible to avoid promoting employment simply through an economy of low skills, low wages and low value-added.

The development of an adaptable 'learning region' calls for cooperation between various local institutions: both formal and informal. Commonly shared habits and values in a given locality, underpinning reciprocal trust and understanding, facilitate cooperation and, ultimately, change. At this juncture, therefore, the learning region is relevant to debates about how to generate social capital (see: Putnam, 1995; Pastor et al., 2000; Maskell, 2001; Trigilia, 2001; Tura and Harmaamkorpi, 2005).

Implications of social capital

Even though definitions of social capital vary (Coleman, 1988; Putnam, 1995; Trigilia, 2001; Meadowcroft and Pennington, 2007), it is generally accepted that the concept refers to associational activity that fosters trust and reciprocity, and hence

---

8   It is essential to note that here the term *collective* should not be seen as referring to those under the government of particular political structures as such. As von Mises pointed out, 'it is always a person who thinks: society does not think, any more than it eats or drinks'. But in this particular context that is to miss the point. *Collective* needs to be associated not with society but with a group of *individuals* who, by interacting with each other, share (tacit) knowledge and thus learn. It is still a *person* who thinks …

cooperation between strangers (Field, 2003: 32). Social capital requires networks of civic engagement between people who are not well known to each other.

Indeed, Jacobs (1961), who coined the term, originally argued that social capital was critical to the success of cities. Tura and Harmaamkorpi (2005) point out, for instance, that social capital plays an important role in creating an innovative capability at regional level. Likewise, Pastor et al. (2000) make a case for 'community-based regionalism', whereby community- and neighbourhood-based advocacy groups cooperate with local elites with a view to ensuring economic growth, social equity and a clean environment. They see local community-building as instrumental to enhancing social capital, which, in turn, lies at the heart of an economically dynamic, socially equitable and environmentally friendly region.

But there is far more to the concept of social capital than that. Not only is it heavy with implications for regional development, but also, crucially, for liberal markets. Some researchers (of left-wing or social democratic orientation) tend to contrast the market with civil society and uncritically regard market forces as undermining the development of social capital in communities. They point out that it is (soulless and uncontrollable) market forces which bring about the atomisation of our societies, which, in turn, risks producing all sorts of undesirable, negative outcomes. These include the weakening of social bonds, the erosion of trust and the destabilisation of democratic governance. Moreover, it is suggested that the failure of some past interventionist policies was also due to the absence of social capital. The state should build social capital first, they argue, then government intervention in the economy would be more effective.

But there is an important, contrary voice. Meadowcroft and Pennington (2007: 24) stress that they believe social capital is important. They argue, 'the operation of a market economy, which involves multiple exchanges between decentralised individuals and organisations, depends in large part upon the existence of trust between market participants'. They further argue that markets themselves are the best institutions for the creation of social capital and civil society. This is because the market, to use Peter Boettke's words, is 'a school of rules, where good behaviour is rewarded, and bad behaviour is penalised. We learn through our experience with markets various habits and values' (in *Foreword* to ibid.: 9). Indeed, trustworthiness, industriousness, promise-keeping and honesty are all qualities that underpin the functioning of the markets and condition long-term value creation: the bankruptcy of Enron, caused by the executives' greed and dishonesty, is a case in point.

It is no coincidence that, as will be demonstrated later on, under communism the quality of social capital was very low (Sztompka, 2002; Hryniewicz, 2007). Indeed, there was little trust among Communist Party officials themselves (who rightly feared Stalinism-style internal purges), between ordinary people and apparatchiks (who suspected the former of plotting to overthrow the regime), as well as among citizens themselves (who often spied on their colleagues and denounced them to the secret police, especially in such countries as East Germany and Romania, where the Stasi and the Securitate had hundreds of thousands of informers). It is, therefore, the communism-imposed lack of market forces and the elimination of political pluralism through one-party rule which wreaked havoc with civil society in central and eastern Europe before 1989 (see also Chapter 7).

The fact that market forces can generate their social capital is an important result. Social capital is important for regional development but that fact alone does not justify interventionist policies.

Critique of the new regionalism and its relevance to central and eastern Europe

The new regionalism and, principally, the concept of the learning region have come in for criticism (see, for instance, Hudson, 1999; Lovering, 1999; MacKinnon et al., 2002; Martin and Sunley, 2003; Purcell, 2004). Purcell (2004: 762) notes that it is problematic to uncritically assume that regions all over the world exhibit similar trends as in Western developed countries. Hence it is equally presumptuous to think that the patterns of regional development as identified in America and western Europe can be easily mimicked in diverse circumstances. The new paradigm seems to bear the characteristics of 'one-size-fits-all' regional policy – that R&D investment and the concept of an adaptable, innovative, 'learning' region are a recipe for success everywhere.

Lovering (1999), drawing on evidence from Wales, highlights the inadequacies of the new regionalism, claiming that the narrative of 'new-regional' development – marked by vague conceptualisation (imprecise definitions and terms) – is detached from reality. In this context, Morgan (1997) illustrated his point through the example of the Welsh Development Agency, which shifted the focus from hard infrastructure to soft infrastructure. Yet the agency was wound up in 2005 and its actual impact on the situation in Wales is hard to unequivocally assess. It is telling that the region is still lagging behind its UK counterparts, most notably in terms of GDP per head (Smith, 2006: 123).

Fundamentally, MacKinnon et al. (2002) claim that, although the focus on knowledge and learning is highly relevant, much of the literature fails to provide empirical inquiry evidence. Similarly, Hudson (1999), while recognising its general importance, suggests that knowledge should not be not treated in a dogmatic fashion. He points to a growing body of literature that examines changes in production and work organisation while placing emphasis on other determinants.[9]

Furthermore, intra-regional business links seem to be over-emphasised at the expense of external linkages (Amin and Thrift, 2002). In this sense, MacKinnon et al. (2002) argue that there is a tendency to underemphasise the significance of wider extra-local networks and structures. Questions are also raised about the rationale for clusters. Martin and Sunley (2003) use the word *chaotic* to describe the concept in its entirety, again underscoring the 'fuzziness' of the definition. To quote one report, 'many, possibly exaggerated, claims are made concerning the existence and economic role of clusters ... Probably many supposed and frequently identified clusters do not exist' (BISER, 2002: 15).

Likewise, it is questioned whether the benefits of close inter-firm cooperation – while indeed of great usefulness to particular sectors – actually 'trickle down to (or across) other sectors' (Purcell, 2004: 763). In the same vein, some hypothesise that knowledge and innovation generated in high-tech clusters are likely to enter the global network rather than be transmitted to

---

9 It is argued that while the UK has been relatively good at 'research' – that is, generating knowledge – compared with the USA, it has been much less successful at 'development' – that is, turning knowledge into commercial advantage.

less technically advanced regions (see also Castells, 2001). This might happen because, as Graham and Marvin (2001) suggest, ICT networks can splinter or polarise places and societies owing to the existence of 'glocal nodes'[10] within cities which link up with similar areas around the world. Given that ICT facilitates interaction and plays down the importance of proximity, innovation generation might increasingly be transferred into and carried out in the global network, benefiting in the first place interconnected large metropolises, with the less developed periphery being progressively marginalised.

Indeed, another tenet of the new regionalism can be doubted – namely, that proximity is intrinsically conducive to learning and innovating. It is suggested people can share – with the help of the same ICT that facilitates technology transfer – tacit knowledge. A case in point is modular work over the Internet, in which several people located in different places around the world collaborate on one project, without actually experiencing the physical presence of their colleagues, yet sharing and exchanging knowledge. Thus physical proximity, albeit of great importance, does not necessarily have to be a *sine qua non* condition for tacit knowledge transmission (see also Breschi and Lissoni, 2001).[11]

Symptomatically, some researchers make a case for non-territorial systems of innovation, in which the territorial dimension

10   In its broadest sense, 'glocal' is used to describe the space where globalisation and localisation meet (see also Swyngedouw, 1989; 1997). More specifically, 'glocal' is often employed to refer to the situation in which local infrastructure assets, while being owned by global entities, are controlled by (nation-state) public regulators (Torrance, 2008, p. 5).

11   Recent work makes a distinction between different dimensions of proximity: geographical, behavioural, technological, industrial and cognitive (see Boschma, 2005; Lang, 2005).

– in contrast to technological or industry criteria – does not play an important part (see Moulaert and Sekia, 2003). At best, it is just a complement. Carlsson and Stankiewicz (1991) define a technological system as a network of vertically and horizontally linked actors and organisations interacting in a given industry to generate, diffuse and apply technological knowledge. It is also argued that innovation generation should be viewed as a *multi-scalar* phenomenon, in which the territory (that is, the regional scale) is just one of the determining dimensions. It follows that innovation processes not only cut across different scales (global, national, regional, local), but also involve non-territorial (sectoral) factors. Oinas and Malecki (1999) capture the multi-scalar nature of innovation in their functional concept of spatial innovation systems, which refers to 'overlapping and interlinked national, regional and sectoral systems of innovation which are all manifested in different configurations in space' (p. 10).

Some think that the role of soft, cultural factors might be overstated, too (Rodrìgues-Pose, 2001). The new regionalism also, arguably, fails to acknowledge the impact of nation-state policies on the fortunes of regions. That problem again bears upon the situation in Poland and other EU-12 states, which, despite being officially recognised by the European Commission as functioning free-market economies, have not totally accomplished the process of transformation.

The new regionalism is – like any comprehensive theoretical approach – vulnerable to criticism. Specifically, the arguments about the role of external linkages and nation-state policies are not easily dismissed. Moreover, regions in different parts of the world indeed do not have to exhibit similar trends – or follow similar developmental paths – as identified in the West.

Yet, the doubts cast over these doctrines and theories, however well founded and insightful, should not be unproblematically accepted either. After all, in some places genuine clusters exist (Cumbers and MacKinnon, 2005). North Carolina, for instance, is now home to 88 biotech companies and approximately one hundred biotech-related businesses. Most of them are located in the so-called 'research triangle', which includes the cities of Raleigh, Durham and Chapel Hill. And clusters can also be found in central and eastern Europe. Let us one more time cite Porter (2007: 20): 'there are literally hundreds of cluster initiatives all over the world today ... there are strong reasons to believe the cluster/region level will be a growing focus of economic policy'. Fundamentally, there is already sufficient empirical evidence that suggests that regions with a higher share of employment in industries that belong to strong clusters are generally more prosperous (European Commission, 2007c: 9).

Modular work over the Internet is a relatively limited phenomenon and hence is unlikely to seriously undermine the necessity of face-to-face contact. It is hard to dispute the importance of flexibility and the need to continually change and adapt to new circumstances. As for the global/national scales of innovation and the use of 'glocal' networks, it is still the case that many small and medium-sized enterprises (SMEs) operate predominantly in the local environment and that it is *their region* which still matters most.

So, despite reservations about some of the ideas underpinning the new regionalism, certain premises of that set of ideas are important and should be an important part of a regional policy framework. The concept of the learning region – regional-scale *learning* and *continual change* coupled with cooperation lubricated by social capital – is of great relevance to *all* Polish regions. It follows that new-regionalism concepts ought to be incorporated into more *eclectic* strategies of regional development.

Whether acceptance of the new regionalism implies a case for any government intervention is a moot point. We shall come to these issues later. It certainly does not, however, provide a case for the form of regional policy that involves 'picking winners' or large cash transfers. What is certainly required, though, is economic liberalisation to facilitate adaptability, so that poor regions can adapt to economic change that arises from membership of the EU and the process of globalisation more generally.

In the next chapter, Poland's regionalism will act as a sort of case study and an illustration of the tendencies and phenomena that are typical of New and Old Europe members alike. The Polish regional agenda acts as a context for analysis of regional problems across the EU. This will allow us both to formulate policy recommendations and, by extension, to discuss the questions of much broader scope that bear upon the European project in its entirety. First, we will look at the character and effects of the systemic transformation in Poland, which, as we will see, has had a profound impact on the picture of Polish regionalism.

7 POLAND'S SYSTEMIC TRANSFORMATION AND ITS IMPACT ON REGIONALISM

We begin with an examination of the results of the systemic transformation of the Polish economy. We highlight the regional implications of national policy and the overall business climate. Special emphasis is placed on the issue of social capital. Poland's regional agenda is then examined to try to understand better the nature and causes of regional disparities.

Poland's stalled reform

Since 1989, Poland, like other ex-communist countries, has undergone a transformation from a centrally planned socialist system to a more free-market economy[1] (Balcerowicz et al., 1997; Balcerowicz, 2003; cf. Siemianowicz, 2006). In the early 1990s, the Polish economy, marked by dynamic growth, falling (though still high) inflation and a relatively friendly business climate, was regarded as a 'tiger' of central and eastern Europe and held up as the best

---

1   In fact, transformation processes began just before the fall of communism. Some say that the beginning of the transformation of the Polish economy can be symbolically traced back to 1988, when a law on economic activity was passed. Authored by Mieczysław Wilczek (the minister of industry in the last communist government), it is justifiably seen as far more liberal than similar laws later enacted after 1989. It is ironic, therefore, that a nominally communist minister was the one who de facto gave Poles the largest degree of economic freedom. As time has passed, however, this freedom has been systematically restricted.

Table 7 **Poland's basic macroeconomic indicators (1990–2007)**

	GDP growth (%) (change on previous year)	Unemployment (%)	Budget balances (% of GDP)	Public spending (% of GDP)	Inflation (%)
1990	−11.6	6.5	0.4	39.8	585.8
1991	−7.6	12.2	−3.8	49.0	70.3
1992	2.6	14.3	−6.0	50.4	43.0
1993	4.0	16.4	−2.8	50.5	35.3
1994	5.2	16.0	−2.7	49.6	32.2
1995	7.0	14.9	−2.6	49.6	27.8
1996	6.0	13.2	−2.5	49.2	19.9
1997	6.5	10.3	−2.5	48.1	14.9
1998	4.3	10.4	−2.6	44.0	11.8
1999	4.0	13.0	−2.1	45.0	10.7
2000	4.1	15.1	−2.7	48.7	11.0
2001	1.0	19.4	−4.5	45.3	5.5
2002	1.5	20.0	−5.1	47.0	1.9
2003	3.7	20.0	−5.0	45.0	0.8
2004	6.9	19.5	−5.3	47,1	4.4
2005	3.2	17.7	−5.0	49.0	0.7
2006	5.8	18.0	−3.9	43.9	1.3
2007	6.4	11.4	−3.0	42.0	2.6

Sources: Central Statistical Office (2008), *Statistical Yearbook 2007*, Warsaw; Central Statistical Office (online), *Statystyki*, Warsaw (accessed 30 January 2008), available at www.stat.gov.pl

example of successful systemic change (see Table 7). Unfortunately, by 2008 that favourable impression seemed to have all but vanished. In sharp contrast to many EU-12 countries that pressed ahead with free-market reform (Slovakia, Romania, the Baltic republics), Poland has evidently gone backwards with regard to the liberalisation agenda.

Ubiquitous red tape, labour market rigidities, high taxes and non-wage labour costs, underdeveloped infrastructure (in bad repair), inefficient courts, obsolete agriculture and powerful vested interests (such as public-sector trade unions) are all impediments to reform. Thus there are now well-substantiated doubts as to whether Poland's decision-makers have wholeheartedly embraced the principles of economic liberalism (Zientara, 2007). In fact, all governments (apart from the first two from 1989 to 1991), disclosing mistrust of the market mechanism and progressively restricting economic freedom,[2] championed – to varying degrees – interventionism and aspired to build a Polish version of the Continental welfare state (Balcerowicz et al., 1997).

All this has found its reflection in Poland's very low places in rankings of competitiveness and business friendliness (Heritage Foundation, 2008; World Bank, 2008; World Economic Forum, 2008a, 2008b). Poland occupies 83rd position in the *Index of Economic Freedom* (Heritage Foundation, 2008) and 51st in the Global Competitiveness Index (World Economic Forum, 2008a). Unsurprisingly, being ranked 76th, Poland fares equally badly

---

2   Whereas many western European parties that are described as 'right-wing' or 'conservative' will tend to favour markets to a greater degree than their socialist counterparts, the Polish right-wing parties tend simply to be socially conservative while in economic policy being anti-market and dirigiste.

for ease of doing business (World Bank, 2008). That not only confirms the view that Polish decision-makers have had little faith in the merits of free-market reform,[3] but also casts a shadow over the country's longer-term development prospects.

Poland has a high unemployment rate. In September 2008 it stood at 9.3 per cent. This was, however, 10.7 percentage points less than the all-time high of 20 per cent at the beginning of 2004. This fall in unemployment was not due to reform, but to economic recovery and, more importantly, to the mass emigration to the UK and Ireland[4] that ensued after Poland's accession to the EU.[5] The root cause of high unemployment is seen in strict employment protection legislation (EPL) and high non-wage labour costs, which discourage job creation (Economist, 2001: 33). The tax wedge[6] (on an average low wage) reached 42 per cent in 2004. Furthermore, high joblessness is accompanied by other adverse labour market trends. Poland has a remarkably low employment rate of workers aged 16–64 (57 per cent). And the employment rate of workers aged 55–64 – at 28.1 per cent (which is 15 percentage points below the EU-27 average) – is the lowest (bar Malta) in the EU (Eurostat, 2008). Compared with countries such

3 Many Polish decision-makers denounce Anglo-Saxon liberalism as socially unjust, forgetting that hundreds of thousands of Poles have voted with their feet, leaving for Britain and Ireland – the European epitomes of market-based capitalism.

4 It is estimated that roughly two million Poles (although estimates vary) emigrated to the UK and Ireland.

5 It is hard to see emigration per se as a negative phenomenon; yet there is a subtle difference between people who leave a country because they want to broaden their horizons and/or get better education and those who emigrate because they cannot find work or are unable to support their families. The mass emigration to the UK and Ireland is a symptom of the latter and is tantamount to the loss of (often first-rate) human capital.

6 The tax wedge is constituted by income tax and social security contributions.

as Sweden (69.6 per cent) and Norway (67.4 per cent), Poland has fared particularly badly in this respect.

The Polish labour market is regulated by the labour code, dating back to 1974, which is deeply rooted in the communist-inspired ideology of a job for life (Zientara, 2008a). According to the OECD (2004: 117), the overall EPL index for Poland totals 2.1, much higher than in the USA (0.7) or the UK (1.1). That the labour code has not so far been seriously modified nor payroll taxes lowered is chiefly down to the activism of trade unions, which – having played a significant role in the demise of the old system – still influence many areas of economic policy.

This is the case despite falling unionisation rates: only approximately 10 per cent of Polish employees belong to a union (Zientara, 2008a).[7] Their power derives from favourable legislation, which is reflected in the high value of the union protection index (UPI). For Poland, the value of the UPI is 0.57, compared with 0.26 for the United States and only 0.19 for the UK (Botero et al., 2004; website dataset). This legislation plays at least as important a part in underpinning union strength as union density (or sheer membership numbers). As Figure 1 shows, union density in Britain is much higher than in France or Poland. Nonetheless, UK unions are no longer as powerful as in the past. In this sense, it is hard to agree entirely with Schnabel and Wagner (2007), who assert that in Europe '[unions'] economic and political power depends on the number of members and on union density' (p. 5).

As strong unions foster labour regulation, the two types of

---

7   Schnabel and Wagner (2007) claim, however, that the figure is 15.7 per cent (p. 8). Note that our computations are based on data provided directly by the public-relations departments of Poland's main trade unions, whereas Schnabel and Wagner's are based on data from the 2002/03 European Social Survey, which might explain the disparity.

Figure 1 **Union density (%)**

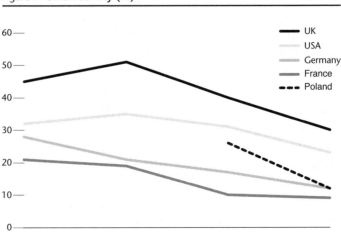

Sources: *Economist*, 'Power without responsibility', 27 April 2006, p. 32; Central Statistical Office (2004), *Polish Statistical Yearbook 2003*, Warsaw; PR departments of Solidarity and OPZZ

regulation – the strictness of EPL and the degree of union protection – tend to go together (Siebert, 2005: 3). This is certainly the case in Poland. Yet, crucially, the anti-reformist activism of trade unions, together with restrictions on hiring and firing procedures, give rise to an insider-outsider labour market, which discriminates against job-seekers and those on temporary contracts or – in the case of Poland – on so-called civil-law contracts.[8] It is interesting,

---

8   In Poland there are two basic forms of employment, regulated by different legislation, so a Pole can be employed under two different regimes. Open-ended contracts and fixed-term contracts are covered by the labour code, whereas so-called 'commission contracts' and 'per-piece contracts' fall under civil law. The latter form of employment grants no protection or entitlements and is used as a way to circumvent the onerous labour code.

Table 8 **Correlations between employment protection legislation and union protection and unemployment**

	Unemployment rate (%)	EPL (0–6)	Union protection index (0–1)
Australia	5.5	1.5	0.37
Austria	5.2	2.2	0.36
Belgium	13.2	2.5	0.42
Canada	7.2	1.1	0.20
Denmark	4.8	1.8	0.42
Finland	8.4	2.1	0.32
France	9.8	2.9	0.67
Germany	11.6	2.5	0.61
Greece	9.8	2.9	0.49
Ireland	4.2	1.3	0.46
Italy	7.7	2.4	0.63
Japan	4.4	1.8	0.63
Netherlands	4.7	2.3	0.46
New Zealand	3.9	1.3	0.25
Norway	4.6	2.6	0.65
Poland	17.7	2.1	0.57
Portugal	7.6	3.5	0.65
Spain	9.2	3.1	0.59
Sweden	6.3	2.6	0.54
UK	4.7	1.1	0.19
USA	5.1	0.7	0.26
Correlation with unemployment	1.0	0.4	0.33

Sources: Unemployment rate, OECD (online), Paris (accessed 12 July 2006), available at: www.oecd.org; EPL, OECD (2004); union protection index, Botero et al. (2004) (website dataset)

therefore, to look at statistical links between EPL, unionisation and unemployment, accepting that, of course, correlation does not prove causation. Table 8 shows that there are positive correlations between EPL, unionisation and unemployment. The link between the strictness of EPL and employment is statistically significant, and Poland fares badly in comparison with the Anglo-Saxon countries.

Despite this, Poland's economic performance has been reasonably good (see Table 7). Economic growth of 6.4 per cent, albeit lower than Latvia's 10.2 per cent or Slovakia's 9.8 per cent, compared favourably with that of Italy or France (around 1–2 per cent). This is, of course, growth from a low base, however, and it is largely due to liberalisation in other areas, including foreign direct investment. The economy still lacks the structural strengths which condition long-term development.

Poland and the challenges of a knowledge-based economy
Economic challenges

Poland ranks low in indicators of the extent of a 'knowledge economy' and indicators of innovation. It is ranked 32nd out of 37 countries on the Summary Innovation Index and 24th out of the 27 EU member states (PRO INNO Europe, 2008: 7). What is more, Poland occupies 72nd place in the Network Readiness Index (Forbes, 2005), which measures the propensity for countries to exploit the opportunities offered by ICT. She lags behind not only all other EU member states except for Bulgaria, but also behind very poor countries such as Ghana or Pakistan.

This should not come as a surprise, given the character of

government redistribution policy, which favours (inefficient and fragmented) agriculture, (loss-making) state-owned heavy industry and (bloated) bureaucracy to the detriment of factors that improve a country's knowledge-based potential. Disproportionate amounts of taxpayers' money are distributed to farmers, industry workers, civil servants and early retirees (Rzońca and Wojciechowski, 2008) in the form of subsidies, tax breaks, debt write-offs and pensions, and this has two effects. It reduces government finance of education, innovation, R&D and ICT. It also reduces private incentives to invest in these fields because factors of production are given incentives to remain deployed in obsolete or low-value-added activities or to remain unemployed. Scientists, teachers and well-educated young people, who embody high-quality human capital, have migrated to other parts of the EU.

In 2007 government spending on R&D amounted to 0.39 per cent of GDP (Figure 2) (PRO INNO Europe, 2008: 40). Tellingly, in the same year, business spending on R&D was only 0.18 per cent of GDP, while only 13.8 per cent of SMEs carried out in-house innovation. Only 8 per cent of the population have broadband access to the Internet (compared with 35 per cent in Denmark). Government support for specific industries, together with employment protection legislation, is discouraging privately led innovation and training in skills relevant to industries in which Poland may have a comparative advantage if resources were not encouraged to remain in unproductive industries.

Furthermore, as primary and secondary education is co-financed both by central government and local administrative units, sometimes in poorer areas (where tax revenues are comparatively low) the quality of teaching suffers. This is particularly

Figure 2   **Government and corporate spending on R&D in selected new member states (2007)**
% of GDP

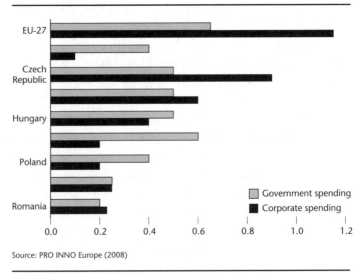

Source: PRO INNO Europe (2008)

evident as far as English and ICT are concerned. Equally importantly, Poland's university education – being 'inward-looking' and 'backward-looking' (OECD, 2008: 46) – is institutionally and mentally still rooted in communism. Rote learning is still favoured, with little stress being placed on individual analysis and creative thinking (conditions *sine qua non* of innovation) or practical skills. In sum, Polish tertiary education is 'insufficiently responsive to the diverse needs of the present-day economy and society' (ibid.: 46).

To summarise, the whole country is neither innovative nor oriented towards technological progress. In the Polish version of a mixed economy priority is given to short-term consumption and maintaining economic resources in unproductive industries. Quite apart from the orientation of government spending, the overall tax burden makes it difficult for private businesses to invest in R&D and human resources development. We now move on to examine the problem of social capital.

Social capital

As the process of learning is interactive and systemic in character, to create an educated and adaptive workforce and commercial sector that is capable of promoting information, there needs to be close cooperation between individuals, corporations, institutions of civil society and, where appropriate, public-sector institutions.[9] This must be lubricated by mutual trust – or social capital. And although, as we have indicated in Chapter 4, the revival of regional civic activism has contributed to reinforcing local social bonds, it is fair to say that the quality of social capital is generally low across Poland (Sztompka, 2002; Grosse, 2006; Zybertowicz and Splawski, 2006; Hryniewicz, 2007, Gardawski, 2007; Jasiecki, 2007). This, as mentioned in the previous chapter, is the legacy of communism, which hampered the formation of social capital in all central and eastern European countries (Grabowska and Szawiel, 2001; Hryniewicz, 2007). It might be instructive to refer to Poland's dramatic history to see what the process of social-capital destruction consisted of.

The Solidarity trade union played a crucial role in the collapse of communism. Its activity is rightly seen as an extraordinary manifestation of social capital: a grassroots movement

9   Even in the more liberal states today, public-sector institutions are involved, rightly or wrongly, with matters to do with planning.

par excellence, uniting blue-collar workers, the middle classes and the intelligentsia in the struggle against a common enemy (Tischner, 1992). Interestingly, in fact, this is the crux of the matter. Generally, it is assumed that social capital is associated with constructing and compromising (that is, with something positive). In a culture of dishonesty, suspicion and corruption – characterised by the absence of social capital – constructive cooperation is much more difficult (see also Hryniewicz, 2007: 29). The social bonds formed in communist times were linked to behaviour associated with *fighting, opposing* and *deconstructing*. Consensus and cooperation were necessary only on a limited basis because the key coordinating characteristic was confronting a common enemy.

In fact, for centuries, the entire Polish society has been pervaded by the spirit of confrontation and polarisation (Sztompka, 2002), by a sort of 'us-versus-them' philosophy that is central to fighting an enemy (Zientara, 2008b). That confrontational and mistrustful attitude has its roots not just in the struggle against communism, but in that against the Nazis and, indeed, the foreign rulers that partitioned Poland in the eighteenth century. Under communism people distrusted the government, while the Communist Party mistrusted ordinary citizens, suspecting them of plotting to overthrow the system, and thus discouraged bottom-up initiative. This is not conducive to consensus-seeking and cooperation, which are part and parcel of a market economy.

Ultimately it was a compromise reached between the communists and the opposition which made it possible to accomplish a bloodless transfer of power (Wałęsa, 1990; Tittenbrun, 1992). Yet that is to miss the point. In fact, shortly after the collapse of the regime, the narrative of conflict and polarisation – coupled with the anti-market rhetoric and calls for more state intervention – began to run through public debate, poisoning not only relations between politicians and citizenry, but also between employers and employees (Grosse, 2006; Zybertowicz and Splawski, 2006), citizens and big business, and so on. This reached its culmination in 2006/07, when the then government launched a campaign to verify who had collaborated with the communist secret police.

What are the ramifications of low rates of social capital for Polish regional policy? If social capital, by enhancing cooperation, plays a critical part in region-level learning and, by extension, regional development, then in Poland the prospects for the implementation of such strategies are not bright. How can a learning region be built if local inhabitants are distrustful, unwilling to compromise and disinclined to cooperate? This problem is thrown into particularly sharp focus in the areas that were home to collective state-owned farms. In those communities social bonds were conspicuously weak and everyday life was marked by over-reliance on the state as a provider of rudimentary welfare, grassroots passivity, overall indifference and mutual mistrust. Little has changed since then. This only confirms the view that whenever market forces – which, as Meadowcroft and Pennington (2007) show, generate their social capital – are seriously restricted or eliminated, 'civicness' and other values collapse.

Poland's regional agenda

As has been mentioned, it is at regional level that disparities between New and Old Europe are particular marked. All Polish regions, or voivodships, are classified as NUT2 regions (bar the capital district of Warsaw; see also Chapter 2, note 2). And, prior

Table 9 Polish regions: basic demographic and socio-economic indicators

	Population (millions) (2006)	Population as % of total (2006)	Urban population (%) (2006)	GDP per capita at current prices (thousands of zlotys) (2005)	GDP per capita in PPS as % of the EU-27 average (2005)	Unemployment (%) (2007)	Households under poverty line, % of total (2005)
Poland	38.6	100	62	25.8	51.3	11.4	23
Dolnośląskie	2.9	7.5	71	26.6	53.0	11.8	26
Kujawsko-pomorskie	2.1	5.4	62	22.4	44.7	15.2	28
Lubelskie	2.2	5.6	47	17.6	35.0	13.0	27
Lubuskie	1.0	2.6	65	23.2	46.2	14.2	19
Łódzkie	2.6	6.7	65	23.7	47.1	11.5	24
Małopolskie	3.3	8.5	50	22.0	43.7	8.8	19
Mazowieckie (capital)	5.2	13.4	65	40.9	81.2	9.2	22
Opolskie	1.0	2.7	52	21.3	42.5	12.0	27
Podkarpackie	2.1	5.4	41	17.8	35.4	14.4	31
Podlaskie	1.2	3.1	59	19.1	37.9	10.7	23
Pomorskie	2.2	5.7	68	25.3	50.4	10.9	17
Śląskie (Silesia)	4.7	12.1	79	27.8	55.3	9.3	17
Świętokrzyskie	1.3	3.3	46	19.3	38.3	15.1	28
Warmińsko-mazurskie	1.4	3.7	60	19.7	39.2	19.0	30
Wielkopolskie	3.4	8.7	58	27.6	54.8	8.0	22
Zachodniopomorskie	1.7	4.3	69	23.9	47.6	16.6	25
Mean	2.39	6.41	59.81	23.64	47.02	12.48	24.06
Standard deviation	1.21	3.07	10.00	5.47	10.85	2.98	4.31

Sources: Author's calculations based on: Central Statistical Office (2005/2006/2007), *Statistical Yearbook of Voivodships*, Warsaw,

Table 10 **Polish regions: selected 'knowledge-economy' indicators (2006)**

	Number of R&D institutions	Total employment in R&D institutions (thousands)	Expenditure on R&D (millions of zlotys)	Gross R&D per capita (zlotys)	Share of businesses with expenditure on innovation (% of total)	Expenditure on innovation in industry (millions of zlotys)
Poland	1,085	121.3	5,893	155	37.3	436.0
Dolnośląskie	81	8.8	298	104	37.2	22.0
Kujawsko-pomorskie	38	4.8	175	85	35.5	8.8
Lubelskie	42	7.2	181	84	37.0	5.3
Lubuskie	18	1.0	24	24	32.9	0.07
Łódzkie	76	7.7	355	138	27.0	18.7
Małopolskie	96	13.4	727	22	37.3	40.2
Mazowieckie	320	33.5	2,463	476	44.1	177.3
Opolskie	21	1.5	36	35	39.0	5.3
Podkarpackie	54	3.1	157	75	43.0	9.4
Podlaskie	21	2.4	61	51	40.1	2.9
Pomorskie	53	6.9	307	139	38.7	24.0
Śląskie (Silesia)	126	11.5	496	106	46.1	79.0
Świętokrzyskie	18	1.2	21	17	32.3	0.7
Warmińsko-mazurskie	16	2.0	55	39	35.6	2.1
Wielkopolskie	88	12.5	455	135	31.8	39.0
Zachodniopomorskie	17	3.6	82	48	26.7	1.6
Mean	67.8	7.6	214.5	98.6	36.5	27.3
Standard deviation	72.9	7.8	202.8	105.6	5.3	43.7

Source: Author's calculations based on: Central Statistical Office (2007), *Science and Technology in Poland in 2006*, Warsaw

to the accession of Romania and Bulgaria, Lubelskie voivodship was the poorest area (on a GDP per capita basis) in the entire Community (see Table 9). One can observe significant disparities between underdeveloped and rich regions within Poland[10] and also between the poorest Polish areas and the richest European ones (within the enlarged Union). The accession of Romania and Bulgaria in 2007 threw the issue into even sharper focus (Begg, 2008: 3).

Regional differences are conspicuous not only in terms of basic economic indicators, but also as far as knowledge-economy potential is concerned (Table 10). While less-developed, peripheral regions are suffering from comparatively high joblessness levels and higher-than-average poverty rates, Poland's biggest cities are booming and function as regional 'poles' of growth. It is there that jobs are being created and wealth generated, not least thanks to the inflow of FDI. Hence core–periphery, urban–rural divides are likely to be reinforced (Zientara, 2008b).

But even if in Polish cities unemployment is comparatively low (and in some labour market segments non-existent), elsewhere – even in many subregions (*powiaty*) situated only 50–100 kilometres from the largest cities – it is over 10 per cent. In the capital region of Mazowieckie there were subregions (such as Makowski and Szydłowiecki) with an unemployment rate of more than 15 per cent (in March 2008). And the situation is worse in the underdeveloped peripheral voivodships in the eastern part

10　The symbolic border between a better-off Poland and a worse-off Poland is the Wisła river. The areas situated to the east of the river, informally called 'Poland B', are commonly associated with agriculture, backwardness and underdevelopment, whereas those located to the west – 'Poland A' – are seen as industrialised, (relatively) modern and developed (with the notable exception of the north-western part).

of Poland and in some areas in the north-west. There unemployment and poverty rates far exceed the national averages and many inhabitants stand little chance of finding employment or do not even look for it. They live off meagre social assistance, which, in turn, perpetuates their dependence on the state and reinforces a feeling of frustration.

The problem is thrown into particularly sharp focus in those subregions (chiefly in Zachodniopomorskie and Warmińsko-Mazurskie voivodships) where under communism state-owned collective farms, mostly inefficient and mismanaged, formed the backbone of local economies. The collapse of the communist regime and the subsequent introduction of market mechanisms laid bare their economic unsoundness. Accordingly, most of them were shut down, which triggered off large-scale redundancies. As a result, thousands of employees, who for years had become accustomed to a socialist work ethos (characterised by little effort and insufficient work commitment coupled with very low labour productivity, low pay and an aversion to change and to new technologies), found themselves simultaneously unemployed and unemployable. This also explains very low rates of social capital – this was not a situation that would naturally engender bonds of trust between individuals and business and between individuals and government. Yet regional disparities, rather than being a recent phenomenon associated with the hardships of the transformation, have their roots in the eighteenth-century partitions (Hryniewicz, 2007: 35) (see Box 2).

Politicians saw an administrative reform as one of the ways to address the regional lopsidedness (Szomburg, 2001). Apart from reinforcing local democracy, this was supposed to prevent the core–periphery, urban–rural divide from growing. Prior to 1999,

Box 2 Implications of the eighteenth-century partitions for today's Polish regions

As a result of the consecutive partitions, carried out in 1772, 1793 and 1795 by Prussia, Russia and Austria, Poland (then a monarchy) lost its sovereignty and ceased to exist as an independent state. Hence in 1795–1918 Polish territories found themselves under the sway of the neighbouring countries. In practice, this meant that all Polish regions had been incorporated into different states and were thereafter ruled, respectively, from Berlin, Moscow and Vienna. So today's western and northern areas became part of Prussia (and later, after 1871, of the unified Germany), southern regions were integrated with Austria (which, after 1848, came to be known as Austria-Hungary), while central and eastern provinces (including territories now in Ukraine and Belarus) were annexed by Russia. This dramatically affected the socio-economic development of particular areas. The places under German rule (especially Silesia) experienced the Industrial Revolution and underwent a period of industrialisation-driven economic growth and dynamic development. In effect, in 1918 – when Poland regained its independence – they turned out to be the most advanced regions in a newly born democratic state. By contrast, the areas under Austrian and Russian sway – with the notable exception of today's Łódzkie voivodship and the district of Warsaw – lagged behind, being just neglected faraway provinces of two ailing empires. They were mainly rural (and agricultural) in character and far less economically developed than the industrialised western regions. In between the wars (1918–1939), regional disparities were not reduced. And after 1945, when Poland again lost its independence, becoming a communist satellite of the Soviet Union, those disproportions persisted (see also Hryniewicz, 2007: 34–42).

Figure 3   Map of Polish regions after the administrative reform in 1999

Source: Author's draft

there existed (under the centralised regime inherited from the communist times) 49 voivodships – too small and economically weak to pursue effectively independent policies appropriate to their own needs. As a result, sixteen larger voivodships came into being in 1999 (Figure 3). The idea was to create fewer but stronger regions, capable of shaping and implementing their local agenda on their own.

Unfortunately, the authors of the reform (owing mainly to political pressure) were not determined to be sufficiently radical.

More responsibility could have been given to regions, especially in the area of taxation and labour market regulation. Experts criticised the number of voivodships and the inadequate extent of devolution. Considering both the historical aspects and the average size of corresponding administrative units in the EU, it is reasonable to claim that six – instead of sixteen – larger, really significant voivodships should have been established. Figure 3 suggests that a more appropriate designation of regional space would have entailed 'merging' the following voivodships: (i) Pomorskie and Zachodniopomorskie; (ii) Lubuskie, Wielko-polskie and Kujawsko-pomorskie; (iii) Mazowieckie, Łódzkie and Świetokrzyskie, (iv) Dolnośląskie, Opolskie and Śląskie; (v) Małopolskie, Podkarpackie, Lubelskie; (vi) Warmińsko-mazurskie and Podlaskie.

Such a designation would have also reflected economic, cultural and historical ties that – in most cases – naturally bind those regions together (Zientara, 2008b). Another argument against setting up so many voivodships and disregarding these natural ties was the resulting diminished capacity of Polish voivodships to make use of EU regional funds (which require co-financing in line with the principle of additionality (Begg, 2008: 8)): bigger regions might potentially have managed to co-finance and hence to implement a greater number of projects. Likewise, in larger regions bigger economies of scale and scope could have been achieved. The establishment of fewer voivodships would also have allowed regions to make substantial administra-tive savings.

As a result, the reform somehow seems to have stopped midway. The effect is a sort of partial decentralisation, in which the designation of regional space tends to cut across the more organic regional economic and cultural structures.[11] This holds true, in particular, in the case of three (now) separate voivodships: Dolnośląskie (Lower Silesia), Opolskie (Opolskie Silesia) and Śląskie (Upper Silesia together with neighbouring areas), which form one historical Silesia region (see also Bafoil, 1999).

The reform also established a regional parliament respons-ible, among other things, for drafting a budget, managing EU funds and carrying out a development strategy. In addition, in each region there is a central government-nominated official (accountable to the prime minister) whose main task is to oversee the functioning of a regional parliament. City mayors, municipal councillors, heads of smaller local administrative units (*gminy* and *powiaty*) as well as regional parliament members are all chosen in direct elections.

The most serious problems affecting Polish regions and subregions are high unemployment and lower GDP per head. The present monograph takes as its premise that what lies at the core of Poland's regional agenda is economic stagnation and socio-technological backwardness of some voivodships and many subregions. This is not to say that regional disparities per se are something inherently wrong. Differences in economic outcomes are a fact of life. Such differences, however, ought not to be too conspicuous and disproportionate (such that they almost imply a gap in the level of civilisation). Also, where differences arise from existing policy arrangements preventing areas from capital-ising on their potential, such impediments should be removed. The underlying point is whether all regions can exploit their

---

11   This has a bearing on the question of whether the choice of regional scale or type actually affects the ability of regions to achieve economic growth (see also Jones and MacLeod, 2004; Marston et al., 2005).

comparative advantage. We believe that the administrative and economic policy framework currently in place in Poland, and most likely in other EU-12 countries too, fails in this respect, which might, among other things, deepen the core–periphery, urban–rural divides.

That is why there is a growing risk that depressed regions, having too little leeway and too few instruments under the present arrangements, are likely to develop at a slower rate and, as a consequence, to lag disproportionately behind booming big cities, which new technology allows to grow as 'glocal' networks, with commercial links to big cities in other countries. Profound change of structural character – potentially running counter to various vested interests – ought to be brought in to reverse the unfavourable trends.

8 PROPOSED POLICY RECOMMENDATIONS

The next three chapters examine policy recommendations aiming both at increasing economic growth in poor regions and at reducing regional disparities where that is appropriate. We begin in this chapter by looking at 'non-solutions' in terms of policies of a more general nature that should be avoided. Then we move on to examine 'non-solutions' in terms of regional policies that should be avoided.

'Non-solutions': general policies to be avoided
Centralisation

Many activist regional policies as well as other central govern-ment interventions principally prevent economic adjustment in depressed regions by imposing rigidities. The principles of labour market regulation, the setting of minimum wages and the provision of welfare payments can be discussed on their own merits. As far as the regional dimension is concerned, however, nationwide regu-lation that does not allow for inter-regional differences in labour productivity or the cost of living can cause long-term unemploy-ment. Although Polish (locally elected) regional authorities enjoy a relatively considerable degree of self-rule, they have no say in setting the minimum wage or social security contributions, which are uniform all over Poland. And this has far-reaching consequences.

Also, if a country – and especially one with a centralised form of government regime – is perceived as being business friendly, on balance its regions are also likelier to be viewed as such. Poland, however, does not fare well in competitiveness and business-friendliness rankings, but, as a 38-million-strong EU member state, has a sizeable market potential and offers a foothold to the entire EU (especially for Asian and American companies). Hence, whenever Poland attracts international capital foreign investors usually decide to locate production and/or create outsourcing jobs in economically strong and more productive regions. This is a reflection of one of the many problems with labour market and business regulation – such regulation tends to affect most detrimentally the least-productive members of society. At the aggregate level, the greatest effect of a general environment of high business and labour market regulation is likely to be high unemployment in the least productive regions. As the actual decision on where to invest is always a complex process whose result depends on many, often *locally specific*, determinants, well-developed voivodships have an edge over poor ones (wage differentials between the core and the periphery in an EU-12 state are – from the perspective of multinationals – not decisive; what really matters is the difference between the cost of labour in the West and in the East).

The peripheral location of less-favoured voivodships, coupled with very bad road infrastructure, lower-than-average per capita GDP and relatively low-quality human capital, renders them less attractive in the eyes of potential investors (Zientara, 2008b).

Regional authorities have too few prerogatives to make themselves look attractive to investment – foreign and local alike (see also Szomburg, 2001). They are unable, for instance, to offer

Table 11 **Special Economic Zones in Poland: basic economic indicators (1994–2006)**

Special Economic Zone	Total investment outlays (billion euros)*	Number of permissions for starting economic activity in an SEZ	Number of jobs generated in SEZ (thousand)
Kamiennogórska	0.3	29	3.2
Katowicka	2.7	126	24.7
Kostrzyńsko-Słubicka	0.4	79	4.6
Krakowski Park Tech	0.1	30	2.4
Legnicka	0.8	46	6.1
Łódzka	0.8	72	6.3
Mielecka	0.8	78	10.8
Pomorska	0.5	42	6.7
Słupska	0.1	30	1.7
Starachowice	0.6	56	3.7
Suwalska	0.1	59	4.0
Tarnobrzeska	0.5	91	8.6
Wałbrzyska	1.6	72	13.9
Warmińsko-Mazurska	0.4	44	3.4
Total	9.7	854	101.1

Source: Author's calculations based on the data provided by the Ministry of Economy; available at: www.mgip.gov.pl/
* In all cases of currency conversion in this monograph, the prevailing rate was 1 euro = 3.4 zlotys.

(potential and actual) local employers lower labour costs. To attract foreign investors, they can only lower local real-estate taxes and conjure up an aura of business friendliness by cutting red tape at the margins. This does not compensate for the productivity differentials between the regions. As a result, richer city regions are being successful at attracting FDI and are becoming richer, while peripheral ones are lagging behind.

To alleviate this problem, in 1994 the then government proposed to establish Special Economic Zones (SEZs). The idea was to grant potential investors special tax privileges in order to encourage them to set up in particularly disadvantaged areas. This was supposed to stimulate economic growth there and thus to reduce joblessness and accelerate the catch-up process. Fourteen SEZs, covering approximately 12,000 hectares, functioned in 2007 (Table 11). It is estimated that in 1994–2006 more than 100,000 jobs were created in these areas. Their functioning – which is frowned upon by the European Commission on competition grounds – is due to end in 2015–17, although there are plans to prolong it to 2025–30.

It is true that the zones have managed to attract much-needed investment and generated a relatively large number of jobs. Yet, as the Commission overtly points out, the rationale of SEZs is open to question. If a given area is designated to be an SEZ, usually this is because of high unemployment and economic retardation. But in the Polish circumstances an area may suffer from a 15 per cent unemployment rate and may not be granted the privileged SEZ status as a 15 per cent unemployment rate is not especially high compared with the national average. Crucially, the decision to establish an SEZ is taken by the Ministry of Economy, which – despite a set of seemingly objective criteria – behaves in an arbitrary fashion. SEZs are therefore a stopgap and not a cure for the regional problem.

From this point of view, the idea of national regional state aid is also open to doubt. The stance of the European Commission is marked by inconsistency. On the one hand, it disapproves of Polish SEZs and, on the other, it finds that national state aid is compatible with the common market (although, to be fair, the Commission does say it has to be used extremely sparingly). In both cases, to encourage potential investors to pursue economic activity in more or less arbitrarily selected areas, the government offers substantial privileges.

Agricultural support

While analysing the potentially harmful effects of various forms of regional support, it is necessary to mention the Common Agricultural Policy (CAP), which accounts for 45 per cent of the EU budget (Esposti, 2008: 14).[1] Even though the CAP is meant to help farmers (that is, it is sectoral rather than geographically based) there is a clear regional dimension to it (Shucksmith et al., 2005). Research has been undertaken into the territorial and regional impact of the CAP in the EU-15 (Laurent and Bowler, 1997; Shucksmith et al., 2005). Although the findings are inconclusive and controversial (Esposti, 2008: 16–17), it is often argued that the Common Agricultural Policy conflicts with the EU's growth objective and is inconsistent with regional cohesion (Tarditi and Zanias, 2001; Rodrìgues-Pose and Fratesi, 2002).

The regional impact of the CAP is likely to be even more significant in central and eastern Europe, where there are far more agricultural areas, which often happen to be poor. Hence the CAP, alongside regional aid for rural areas (see below), will indirectly affect national- and local-level efforts to deal with the growing urban–rural divide. In Poland, irrespective of whether direct payments will actually translate into a higher regional GDP per capita, the CAP is set to have a negative effect on the local economic base. This is because subsidies are bound to conserve

---

1   The CAP costs European taxpayers over €40 billion a year, or around 45 per cent of the EU budget (Esposti, 2008: 14). That is a huge sum, given that farming accounts for less than 2 per cent of the EU's workforce.

the fragmented structure of the country's agriculture (Chaplin et al., 2007), at the same time fostering dependence on the state as a provider of welfare and, critically, acting as a disincentive to change.[2] This, in turn, risks, among much else, slowing down the diversification of local economic activity.

Many farmers who possess tiny plots receive direct income payments from the EU taxpayer, which induces them to keep cultivating their land, even though there is no economic rationale to do so. It discourages farmers from selling their plots and looking for other jobs. Admittedly, high unemployment and lack of skills do not help either since those considering giving up their subsistence farming simply have few prospects for alternative employment (ibid.). In addition, given that all farmers are exempt from paying income tax and pay far lower social security contributions, they are de facto subsidised by the Polish taxpayer – and by other industries in the poor regions. As mentioned above, in the worse-off rural areas hit by closure of collective farms, all this has bred passivity and degradation.

In 2006, within the framework of the CAP, approximately 1.4 million Polish agricultural households received 7.8 billion zlotys (against 6.6 million zlotys in 2005).[3] The agricultural land entitled to the subsidies covered 13.7 million hectares (92.8 per cent of total cultivated land). Specifically, a Polish farmer was given 276 zlotys for each (uncultivated) hectare and 313 zlotys for each

---

2   This fragmented structure of the Polish agricultural sector has its roots in a post-war agricultural reform, whereby all private land was first confiscated and nationalised, and then – in the name of socialist justice – earmarked for the creation of collective farms and redistribution to individual smallholders.

3   In Slovakia 70 per cent of the population live in rural areas, but only 5 per cent is engaged in agricultural activity. By contrast, in Poland the respective figures are approximately 30 per cent and 18 per cent.

wheat-planted hectare (note, for the sake of comparison, that the minimum gross monthly wage in 2007 was 936 zlotys). In relative terms, the amounts Polish farmers received constituted 65 per cent of the EU-15 average. Of course, in Poland, as in other EU countries, it is farmers holding the largest plots (that is, usually the most affluent ones) who are the biggest beneficiaries of the CAP.[4]

In addition to that, many Polish farmers will receive support from the Rural Development Programme, financed by the European Agricultural Fund for Rural Development[5] (EAFRD) (Meisinger, 2006). Within the framework of the Rural Development Programme, which targets three core objectives by means of 41 detailed measures, €17 billion will be earmarked for Polish rural areas in 2007–13, of which one third will be spent on the promotion and development of ecological farming.

Notwithstanding the existence of a few modern farms which successfully export Polish produce abroad (Zięba and Kowalski, 2007), the fragmented agricultural sector in its entirety is generally regarded as inefficient and outdated (Chaplin et al., 2007). From a certain point of view, agriculture is, like the coal industry and the public health service, a relic of real socialism. And the CAP, being par excellence socialist in character, helps to maintain the status quo. Yet abolishing the CAP (or at least modifying its principles) – which falls completely under the purview of the EU – will be fiercely opposed both by France, the single biggest beneficiary, and Polish farmers' trade unions. As a consequence,

---

4 In France over a quarter of payments go to just 5 per cent of the farmers. It is calculated that the biggest thirty farmers (among them, Prince Albert of Monaco) get an average of over €390,000 each a year.

5 Note that rural areas cover 90 per cent of the EU's territory and are home to around 50 per cent of its population.

the stigma attached to Polish rural subregions – commonly seen as backward, retarded and economically sluggish – is unlikely to be removed soon.[6]

'Non-solutions': regional policies to be avoided

Let us now turn to regional policies to be avoided. As Smith (2006) demonstrates, government-led welfare redistribution from richer to less prosperous regions risks having damaging effects on local employment and output (pp. 119–37). This sort of assistance can equally be harmful to the entire economy by entrenching vested interests and leading potential entrepreneurs to engage in rent-seeking rather than wealth-creating. Poland is a country with the largest number of regions (thirteen out of sixteen) in which disposable income exceeds the primary income. As Poland is characterised by high GDP per capita disparity, this may imply that wealth is generated mainly in a few economically

6   Nonetheless, irrespective of the future course of CAP reform, some measures to restructure Poland's agriculture (for which, as mentioned above, money will be available from the Rural Development Programme) could be taken. This would entail the elimination of the above-mentioned fragmentation and, consequently, the consolidation of land and the creation of far bigger, highly specialised, farms which – thanks to economies of scale and the good reputation of Polish food – could successfully vie with their western European counterparts (Chaplin et al., 2007). A step in the right direction would be to speed up the process of granting elderly farmers EU-funded structural pensions in return for their tiny plots. The land would then be taken over by a state agency (and/or by their children) and resold to farmers willing to expand their acreage, which, in turn, would be conducive to consolidation. This might also be attained through the bottom-up formation of farmers' cooperatives with a view to cutting costs and enhancing efficiency. On the other hand, the development of smaller-scale higher-margin ecological farming, for which financial resources are also available, would need to be intensified. At the moment, the payment of subsidies and transfer payments provides no incentives for consolidation or efficiency.

strong regions that end up subsidising the underdeveloped periphery.

These policies are connected with the 'old regionalism', whereby the state supports with taxpayer's money loss-making sectors (especially heavy industry), located mainly in traditional industrial regions. In Poland such assistance was granted, among others, to state-owned coal mining, steel making and ship-building – all heavily unionised. The coal sector, with almost all pits located in Silesia, received (in 1990–2003) 63 billion zlotys (in 2002 prices) in all forms of aid – direct subsidies, debt write-offs, tax exemptions, early retirement schemes, etc. Even though so much money had been pumped into the industry, in 2007 it was not economically sound. Undoubtedly, such policy fostered the culture of 'corporatism', whereby the most powerful professional groups force governments to yield to their financial demands.

With the availability of EU pre-accession and post-accession regional aid at the beginning of this decade, the shift from Warsaw-led to Brussels-led redistribution began. The Commission's tight control of the legality of state aid also played a part in this shift. As things stood in 2008, the financial assistance allocated from the central budget to regions in the form of so-called 'voivodship contracts' constituted a minor part of the total regional aid, which comes chiefly from the EU.[7] But the problem resurfaced in a different guise. As Brussels money comes to regions indirectly via Warsaw – where Polish civil servants both allocate resources to individual voivodships and approve so-called

---

7 In 2002–06, for example, Pomorskie voivodship received €2.8 billion, of which only €240 million came from the central budget. In addition, all Polish regions (bar the capital district of Warsaw) qualify for national regional state aid.

Regional Development Strategies[8] – there has been heated debate on whether to direct more financial resources to economically strong core regions (which, functioning as poles of growth, would then drive nationwide socio-economic development) or to under-developed eastern regions.

This is a multifaceted, contradiction-ridden issue. For one thing, it is argued that some of the European money might be wasted as the eastern periphery is not fully (technically) prepared to deal with such considerable resources. This was borne out by the fact that some authorities from the eastern voivodships had substantial difficulties coming up with coherent 2007–13 Regional Development Strategies and almost missed the deadline for their submission. It has to be said, however, that much needs to be done in terms of infrastructure improvement to bridge the gap between eastern regions and other regions of Poland.

It is certainly clear that regional aid, of itself, is not going to be the driver of growth and that it might well foster institutions and attitudes that prevent poor regions from growing. The capacity of the central Polish government to handle regional aid has also been found wanting. If regional aid is to have any beneficial effect then it should be accompanied by devolution to regions. To some extent, the inflow of EU money is somewhat forcing coop-eration on local actors, thereby promoting qualities and patterns of behaviour (compromise-seeking, collaboration, integrated problem-solving) that underpin the build-up of social capital and strengthen the formation of local identity.

---

8   It has to be said, though, that regional authorities can receive some financial resources directly from Brussels within the framework of Regional Operational Programmes (ROPs). An ROP, listing the proposals of investment projects in a given voivodship, is prepared by local authorities and sent directly to the European Commission for approval.

It follows that European regional policy constitutes a complex and multifaceted issue that – especially in central and eastern Europe – needs to be conceptualised in different contexts. The next chapter analyses the effectiveness of EU cohesion policy through a review of the literature and examination of the evidence from other EU countries. It is possible in theory that some types of regional aid might be helpful, but it is by no means clear that the disadvantages do not outweigh the advantages.

9 EU REGIONAL AID AND EVIDENCE FROM OTHER MEMBER STATES

This chapter focuses on the effectiveness of EU regional aid. This is done through a review of the literature and examination of the evidence from selected member states, namely Ireland, Spain, Germany and Romania.

General assessment of the effectiveness of European cohesion policy

Given the emphasis the EU places on regional convergence and the financial resources it earmarks for this objective, it is pertinent to investigate the effectiveness of European cohesion policy. In other words, has EU regional policy fulfilled its overarching objective of contributing to reducing regional disparities in GDP per capita?[1] This has been the subject of much debate since the first programming period of Structural Funds (1989–93). In this context, Esposti (2008: 14) points out that:

> … it may be surprising to realise after almost 20 years that empirical evidence on [cohesion policy's] impact is still controversial and, in fact, incomplete. Whether growth

---

[1]   It is important to remember, however, that European cohesion policy has historically addressed – apart from its overarching goal of reducing disparities – three objectives: (1) promoting European *legitimacy*; (2) improving overall *competitiveness*; (3) increasing citizens' *equity* (De Michelis, 2008: 10).

convergence really occurred in the EU and whether *cohesion policy* played a significant positive role in this respect is an empirical question, to which no conclusive answer can be provided at the moment.

It emerges from the Commission's Fourth Cohesion Report (European Commission, 2007b) that convergence can be observed both at national and regional levels (but, at the same time, it identifies – in line with what has been argued in Chapter 2 – progressing regional divergence within many member states). Yet a number of studies find little evidence that cohesion policy increases growth rates (Ederveen et al., 2006; Santos, 2008) or that it has a positive impact on the convergence process (Abraham and Van Rompuy, 1995; Molle and Boeckhout, 1995). All this suggests that regional subsidies may be much less useful than European officials seem to believe (Funck and Pizzati, 2003; Sapir et al., 2004).

In fact, cohesion policy appears to function as a second-best substitute for labour mobility. In other words, 'it can help bring jobs to people in backward areas, when people in those areas will not go to the jobs' (Cottrell, 2003: 11). Yet this is achieved at a cost to efficiency since it encourages businesses to make investments where they would not otherwise have made them. In other words, European cohesion policy, as Santos (2008) notes, pursues conflicting objectives by allocating resources to regions where returns on capital are low. It might thus help reduce regional disparities, but at a cost to national growth.

That said, some macroeconomic modelling studies present a more sanguine view, 'partly because they attempt to look beyond the immediate effects' (Begg, 2008: 5). Bradley et al. (2007), while analysing the mechanism of regional aid, discern two phases: in an initial, 'implementational time phase', subsidies affect a local economy mainly through the demand side (demand is boosted by, for example, construction and renovation); later improvements in infrastructure and/or human capital give rise to 'supply-side' effects. The European Commission seems to reason along similar lines. In one of its reports on social and economic cohesion, it argues that:

> ... transfers from the Structural Funds added directly to demand and economic activity, but more importantly, since they were concentrated on investment ..., they were aimed at increasing growth potential in the medium and long term ... The estimates of the 'supply-side' effects on growth ... become predominant in the long term ... Although structural polices are ultimately judged in terms of their effect in narrowing regional disparities in GDP per head of employment, it is their impact on the underlying factors which determines economic development. (Cited in Esposti, 2008: 15)

But these 'supply-side' effects need to be reinforced by more profound change. Hence Structural Funds are likely to produce most beneficial outcomes if they are combined with free-market reform. They are, indeed, best used to improve transport, ICT, power and water infrastructure as well as to upgrade human capital via education and training. Such uses of regional aid, as they are not inherently discriminating in favour of or against particular industries, yield benefits that are on balance far more lasting than if they are used to finance, for instance, schemes designed to back the development of particular small and medium-sized enterprises. Nonetheless, if simultaneously nothing is done to ameliorate a poor nationwide business climate then the EU taxpayer's money will mostly be wasted.

Indeed, ultimately it is national policies, in particular in taxation and labour market regulation, which condition a region's attractiveness to investment. Subsidies may, therefore, be ineffective and even counterproductive, if – by masking the long-term effects of mistaken government policies – they weaken decision-makers' determination to introduce structural change. Besides, as public choice economics suggests, regional aid can also orientate entrepreneurial activity upwards towards those providing grants rather than to creating wealth. It also produces client groups that have a vested interest in more state activity as well as diverting the attention of regional and national government away from their proper day-to-day business towards obtaining grants, and justifying earlier grants, given by higher levels of government.

In trying to separate the various strands of policy that are important for development, it is informative to examine the experience of countries that have been major recipients of regional support. Specifically, in the following sections, we will examine how Ireland, Spain and East Germany made use of the EU's vast financial resources. In addition, we refer to Romania, albeit – given that it joined the EU only in 2007 – for a different purpose. There are certain similarities between these countries and Poland.

Success stories: evidence from Ireland and Spain

Ireland was one of three countries that were admitted to the then EEC in the first wave of new entrants (the UK and Denmark were the others). In 1973 Ireland was a poor Catholic country with an obsolete economic structure (a large agricultural sector). At that time many Irishmen, like many Poles today, were leaving their motherland for the USA, the UK and elsewhere in search of employment and brighter prospects. Ireland did not start to experience fast economic growth until the late 1980s, when the then government – not least thanks to the cooperation of trade unions, which agreed to sign the so-called social pact in 1987 (Zybała, 2006: 57–8) – pressed on with nationwide liberalisation. The reform was accompanied by the effective use of European regional aid, which was used in a way that helped to enhance the country's productivity. Ireland, unlike Greece, did not 'consume' EU financial resources, but, broadly, spent those resources on ICT and road infrastructure and R&D, which – in line with the above reasoning – produced 'supply-side' effects. This, in turn, helped to attract FDI, including the capital brought by many re-emigrants who decided to return.

In consequence, Ireland has become one of the richest countries in the EU (with a GDP per capita of almost $44,000, it now comes second behind Luxembourg and, with an average rate of growth of 5 per cent per annum in 2000–06, it is one of its most dynamic old members).[2] Ireland enjoys virtually full employment, with one in ten workers now a foreigner (many from Poland). In every Irish region GDP per capita in PPS is well above 75 per cent of the EU-25. Ireland is also characterised by the lowest GDP per capita disparity (a factor of 1.6) in the entire Community. Likewise, regional labour productivity is higher than the EU average. In sum, Ireland is perceived as a success story and held up as a good

2 In 1988 Ireland's GDP per head was 15 per cent above that of Portugal, but Ireland's GDP per head in 2008 was double that of Portugal, even though both countries have enjoyed comparable support from the Structural Funds (Begg, 2008: 3).

example of how a country can spectacularly reinvent itself with the help of the right policies (Munkhammar, 2007: 117–21).

Admittedly, Ireland is endowed with a number of inherent advantages that facilitated this reinvention. Its economy is comparatively small and it is arguably easier to reform smaller-sized systems. It has an English-speaking population and a rich, influential diaspora in America, willing not only to invest in Ireland, but also to lobby in defence of its interests. This is not to belittle the magnitude of the success, which is mainly due to the adoption of a consistent strategy that combined liberalisation and EU aid.

There are even more analogies between Spain and Poland. Spain, admitted to the EEC together with Portugal in 1986, had experienced, like Poland, a long period of dictatorship. This meant that both countries – having roughly comparable territories and populations – first had to restore democracy and put into place the institutional framework[3] indispensable to the proper functioning of the market. Furthermore, Spain resembles Poland in that it is formally Catholic and has a similar number of sizeable regions (seventeen). When the old regime came to an end, many of the newly created *comunidades* – in particular, rural ones in the interior – were extremely poor. But the regional disparities are now much less conspicuous than two or three decades ago.

But here the similarities end: in Spain the system of national governance is much more decentralised than in Poland. As a result, Spanish regions enjoy more autonomy than their Polish counterparts (the Spanish *comunidades* control some 36 per cent

---

3   Institutions such as regulators, supervisory bodies and politically independent courts, which are sometimes described as 'institutional thickness' (De Michelis, 2008: 11).

of public spending). It follows that they have much more leeway in shaping and pursuing their development agenda. That is not to suggest, of course, that Poland's relationship between the centre and the regions should be modelled on the Spanish one: in Spain the cultural and historical differences between *comunidades autónomas* are much more pronounced than in Poland. Nonetheless, more power devolution from the centre to the regions (resulting in higher degrees of self-rule) would definitely constitute a step in the right direction.

During the decade that followed accession (1986–96), Spain – despite introducing a relatively bold programme of privatisation and deregulation – made less progress than expected. Under the socialist government of Felipe González, unemployment topped 20 per cent, inflation was high and budget deficits kept rising. Even though the socialists managed to restructure Spain's inefficient heavy industry, they failed both to cut public spending and, equally importantly, to liberalise the labour market and weaken the power of trade unions.

It was only after the government of José María Aznar carried through free-market reform – in particular, in the area of labour law – that economic growth accelerated. This coincided with the massive inflow of EU regional aid, which was again used for infrastructure, as in the case of Ireland, to help connect rural areas with booming agglomerations. Prior to the entry of the ex-communist countries, Spain – alongside Ireland, Portugal and Greece – was the largest recipient of EU assistance. It is estimated that in 1986–2006 Spain received net transfers of €93.3 billion (at 2004 prices), the equivalent of an extra 0.83 per cent of GDP growth each year for twenty years (Rennie, 2008: 10).

With Poland and other eastern European states nearing

accession, the Spaniards knew that the lion's share of the Structural Funds would be shifted to the east. But in recent years Spain has experienced a period of dynamic growth (double the euro zone average), falling unemployment (to 8–9 per cent) and rising living standards. This allowed Spain to reduce markedly the development gap between it and more prosperous EU-15 countries. Unsurprisingly that favourable state of affairs has had a profound impact on the situation in Spanish regions. Although fairly significant regional differences in terms of GDP per capita and labour productivity still exist (in two regions – Andalusia and Extremadura – GDP per inhabitant is below 75 per cent of the EU-25 average), the catching-up process continues to proceed at a relatively fast pace. At the same time, we can notice the same tendency of large metropolitan areas (Madrid, Barcelona, Valencia) to develop fastest and hence to act as engines of economic growth.

East Germany and the pitfalls of reunification

East Germany, in contrast, offers a different tale. The country was the first ex-communist state to have joined the EEC through reunification with West Germany in 1990. Despite being slightly better developed than Poland, just before the fall of the Berlin Wall, East Germany's economy – mismanaged during four decades of communist rule – was equally inefficient and economically unsound. Hence the incorporation threw into sharp focus the huge development gap between the western and eastern *Länder*. Not surprisingly, it immediately turned out that an average inhabitant of the prosperous west (*Wessi*) was several times as wealthy as an average easterner (*Ossi*). This made the creation of one Germany look like attaching or 'gluing' the poor East to the affluent West, rather than reunifying the two parts. This, in turn, highlighted the need to adopt a policy that could speed up the catching-up process.

In the event, this policy took the form of vast financial transfers from the western regions to the eastern ones. All this took a heavy toll on the economy in general and the state of the public finances in particular. At the same time, with the symptoms of euro-sclerosis intensifying (an annual growth of 1–2 per cent, unemployment exceeding 10 per cent),[4] voices were raised to push ahead with free-market reform. Yet, despite some attempts to make the labour market more flexible (known as the 'Hertz IV' reform), little was achieved as the powerful vested interests (mainly trade unions) forced the governments of Gerhard Schröder and Angela Merkel to back down (though labour organisations did restrain their wage demands).

The experience of East Germany clearly demonstrates that pouring considerable amounts of money into depressed regions while shunning structural change is not the right solution. Since reunification, a total of €1.3 trillion has been pumped into the East with a view to accelerating its integration with the rest of the country; currently the eastern *Länder* receive transfers of €80 billion a year – about 4 per cent of Germany's GDP (Siegele, 2006: 5). This becomes evident if we compare GDP per capita and disposable income in eastern regions. Whereas the majority of East Germany's *Länder* have GDP per inhabitant below 82 per cent of the EU-25 average, in all of them disposable income per household in PPCS is between €10,000 and €15,000

---

4   As we remember from Table 5, the East German region of Mecklenburg-Vorpommeren had the highest unemployment rate in the entire EU (17.4 per cent) in 2007.

– a comparatively high value by EU-27 standards (in Romanian regions, for instance, it is far below €5,000). Hence the spatial redistribution of German national income produces a double 'enriching and levelling' effect.

Even so, the overall results of the transfers are unconvincing and the policy is thought of as counterproductive, if not wasteful. High welfare benefits act as a disincentive to work, fostering passivity and reliance on the state. New roads and refurbished buildings might be necessary, or at least provide positive returns on investment, but are insufficient to ensure entrepreneurial dynamism, a prerequisite of fast-paced economic convergence. Without cutting red tape, easing EPL and lowering payroll taxes, it was naive to expect that income transfers alone could possibly lay the foundations of a vibrant local economy likely to guarantee long-term economic growth and successful social development. Moreover, a generally lower quality of social capital in the East than in the West (the legacy of communism) plays a part, too.

East Germans are generally considered far less entrepreneurial than Poles. While Polish areas situated near the border buzz with small-scale economic activity (low-end services such as hairdressing thrive since many Germans, attracted by low prices, cross the border to have their hair cut or their teeth filled),[5] neighbouring districts on the other side of the Oder river are stagnant. There is a lower quality of human capital in the East than in the West (in terms of skills and a work ethos). It comes as no surprise,

5   This is consonant with economic theory which says that, when economies at different stages of development undergo an integration process, prices of tradable goods tend to get harmonised first. In contrast, prices of non-tradable goods (say, haircuts) get harmonised far more slowly. Hence the differences in prices of many services are a de facto testament to real convergence disparities.

then, that East German workers are still much less productive than their western colleagues (although their productivity is a little higher than that in other EU-12 countries). As a result, high non-wage labour costs discourage low-end job creation in the eastern *Länder*. Unlike in the western regions, they are not offset by high productivity rates.

But that problem has more profound implications. When deciding on where to locate investment, a potential foreign or national investor is likely to discriminate against East Germany. A few kilometres eastward (in Poland or the Czech Republic), they can benefit from far cheaper labour, whose productivity, albeit lower than in East Germany, is going up rapidly (especially in manufacturing). In other words, its ex-socialist neighbours – by offering relatively low-cost labour which more than compensates for slightly lower productivity – undercut East Germany and thus stand more chance of attracting much-needed FDI. East German labour costs are raised and underpinned by social security transfers, effectively from western taxpayers.

It follows that East Germany risks missing out on the opportunities offered by globalisation and European integration. Relocation of production and service outsourcing from the high-cost West to the low-cost East might actually pass it by. It is true that some areas in the eastern *Länder* have attracted investment (for instance, the urban districts of Jena and Dresden) and are developing at a relatively fast pace, but the fact remains that it was thanks to classic SEZ-like enticements or political pressure (Volkswagen in Dresden). Other regions, in particular in the north, seem to be lagging behind. In Mecklenburg-Vorpommeren and Brandenburg GDP per capita in PPS is below 75 per cent of the EU-25 average. In 1999–2003 in most eastern *Länder* GDP per inhabitant actually decreased by five percentage points compared with the EU average (Eurostat, 2006: 33).

In short, East Germany fell into a trap. A generous western welfare state – with its high social benefits, heavy taxation and strictly regulated product and labour markets – was somehow 'grafted' on. And that was the last thing East Germany needed as the Continental social model is seen as the root cause of the malaise of the biggest euro-zone economies (sluggish economic growth, low employment rates, unsustainable budget deficits). Instead of following in the footsteps of most ex-communist countries that have reformed their economies along Anglo-Saxon lines – which soon translated into dynamic economic growth and low unemployment – East Germany was burdened with a system that neither encourages job creation nor promotes socio-economic advancement.

Latvia and Estonia – the ex-soviet republics that for 40 years belonged to the same bloc as the former German Democratic Republic – are growing at above 10 per cent a year. Compared with that, the dynamism of East Germany's regional economies is unimpressive, to say the least. Furthermore, while in the Baltic republics few people stay out of work for any period, in the eastern regions of Germany unemployment is double the (already high) national average. Worse, from a sociological point of view, high joblessness, coupled with generous unemployment benefits and low (trans-border) labour mobility,[6] not only breed violent behaviour among an idle and frustrated youth, but also foster

6   In sharp contrast to Poles, who flooded into the UK in search of employment after 1 May 2004, East Germans did not find it attractive to look for work on the other side of the Channel even though they were allowed to work in the entire EU long before 2004. Note that in 2004 unemployment rates in most Polish regions and eastern *Länder* alike exceeded 20 per cent.

xenophobia. This has been borne out by the electoral successes of the neo-Nazi parties in the East.

Romania's economic agenda and lessons for Poland

It is the combination of free-market reform and the appropriate use of regional aid coupled possibly with an improvement in human and social capital which has seemed to promote growth in poor regions. In other words, if regional assistance is to be effective, the implementation of EU-financed projects has to be accompanied by nationwide liberalisation. In this sense, Romania, in contrast to Poland, appears to be heading in the right direction. This Balkan country, which joined the EU in the last wave, has a comparable size and demography to Poland. It is still less affluent than Poland, and all of its regions (except the capital region of Bucharest) are poor even by central and eastern European standards. They lag far behind their EU counterparts in terms of GDP per capita and productivity levels.

Nonetheless, it is the Romanian government, not the Polish one, which decided to press on with sweeping economic reform (introducing a low flat-tax regime, cutting red tape, tackling corruption, reforming the judiciary, etc.) and it is Romanian regions, not Polish ones, which have developed more dynamically (albeit from a lower base) and have experienced the highest increases in GDP per capita (Eurostat, 2006: 33).[7] Romania (47th place) ranks higher than Poland (76th) in the ease-of-doing-business ranking (World Bank, 2008) and in the Index of Economic Freedom (Romania is in 68th position and Poland

---

7   On average, in 2000–06 the Romanian economy grew by more than 5 per cent a year.

in 83rd) (Heritage Foundation, 2008). The World Bank (2008) ranked Romania second in the world in terms of the progress the country had made to ensure an investor-friendly environment. Symptomatically, in January 2008 Nokia decided to relocate its factory from Bochum in Germany to Cluj in Romania (Rennie, 2008: 4).

Apart from the market potential, Poland's greatest advantage – especially for western European manufacturers that shift production from high-cost Germany or France – lies mainly in relatively low labour costs and, thanks to geographical proximity, low transport costs. The availability of a comparatively well-skilled workforce in such regions as Śląskie plays a part, too. Yet the cost of Polish labour is low only in relation to EU-15 wages. In the longer run, relying only on wage differentials could prove a short-sighted strategy, given that Romania and most central and eastern European countries (Latvia, Lithuania, Ukraine, Estonia) – not to mention India and China – have lower wages than Poland and a growing pool of well-educated and high-skilled labour. It follows that if other countries from central and eastern Europe single-mindedly continue to liberalise their economies they are bound to be more successful in attracting FDI than Poland.

In other words, even though today Poland's cities and richest regions see jobs being generated by the inflow of foreign capital, tomorrow these jobs risk being transferred farther east or south.[8] Indeed, even medium-sized Polish enterprises – in an attempt both to remain competitive and to skirt a constantly worsening

---

8   In 2000–06 Poland's southern regions lost out to Slovakia and the Czech Republic while trying to attract such international car producers as Toyota, PSA and Hyundai. It is true that Toyota set up an engine/gearbox factory in Wałbrzych in Dolnośląskie region, but the fact remains that its car plant was located in the Czech Republic.

business climate – are increasingly shifting (low-end) production to China and Ukraine.

To recapitulate, it transpires that the successful way to transform poor regions is to combine free-market reform with regional aid that is used to build/renovate infrastructure rather than encourage unproductive industries to locate in poor regions. The quality of local HR practices and social capital is also important. The evidence from East Germany suggests that throwing money at less prosperous areas without structural and cultural change or while burdening them with excessive regulation and heavy taxation is a recipe for failure.

In the following chapter we present strategies that need to be followed with a view to transforming the fortunes of Poland's depressed regions: though the policy suggestions could easily be adapted to other regions in 'New Europe'.

10 STRATEGIES FOR REINVIGORATING THE REGIONS

This chapter argues for the adoption of a strategy that is premised on political decentralisation and economic liberalisation. Such a policy would enable rich and poor regions alike to make best use of their comparative advantages. The chapter presents specific policy recommendations and provides – by concentrating on real-life examples – an explanation of what in practice the mechanism of change in Poland could consist of. The final section provides a brief case study from Silesia, which bears some of the characteristics of a learning region. We stress the role of social capital in regional development. It is important to point out that the conclusions can be generalised. These strategies can be followed in all EU-12 countries. Indeed, many of them have been derived from lessons learnt in other countries.

Liberalisation

All post-communist countries need to follow a strategy of liberalisation. Poland, in particular, urgently needs to improve its business environment to ensure development in poor regions. The fact that Poland comes very low among other EU member states in business-friendliness and competitiveness rankings bears witness to its structural weaknesses. It has lost its status as 'a tiger' of central and eastern Europe and urgently needs economic liberalisation. Poland helps to explain why backtracking on free-market reform hinders entrepreneurship and hampers long-term development. The country, in other words, is a showcase of the ineffectiveness of misguided (and populist) interventionism. With high unemployment and mass emigration, it represents an example of missed opportunities and wasted potential.

The importance of liberalisation to the regions cannot be underplayed. Illiberal business and labour market policies tend to have the effect of making factors of production less productive as well as reducing entrepreneurial activity. It is the least productive individuals and regions which are likely to suffer most from this as productivity falls below the levels of income achievable from social security systems.

The economy's relatively good performance in 2006 and 2007 should not be seen as a sign of strength or as a harbinger of change. On the contrary, the upturn, mainly cyclical in character, had a perverse effect on reformist efforts and allowed politicians to defer making unpopular decisions. Worse, it prompted a union-led escalation of pay demands, which coincided with the wage inflation in those segments of the labour market where the labour shortages resulting from the mass outflow of skilled workers to the UK and Ireland were most acute.

Thus the question of nationwide free-market reform comes to the fore. Instead of setting up new SEZs, which distorts the allocation of resources, Poland could be declared a single SEZ by introducing a flat tax, lowering non-wage labour costs (thereby reducing the tax wedge), cutting more red tape and easing strict EPL (thus rendering the labour market more flexible). This, of course, should be accompanied by a profound reform of the public finances (which, in turn, would entail reducing public spending and overhauling retirement arrangements) and by a viable privatisation programme (which would relieve the budget of loss-making state-owned enterprises).

One of the main obstacles to public finance reform – the lack of which is, itself, a huge obstacle to raising the productivity of 'old' regions – is the state social security system. The main components of the national pension system are the nationwide pay-as-you go scheme (ZUS), and the (separate) farmers' pension fund (KRUS). Both ZUS and KRUS – beset by the constantly rising deficits due to the disproportionate number of early pensioners and disability-benefits claimants as well as the huge cost of farmers' pensions – are annually subsidised with billions of zlotys. In 2006, for instance, ZUS had a deficit of 34.3 billion zlotys (which is expected to rise to 50 billion zlotys in 2020) (Rzońca and Wojciechowski, 2008: 21). Likewise, in 2007 KRUS had a deficit of 16 billion zlotys. It is estimated that in 2000–07 the annual cost of all sorts of early retirement schemes amounted to 2.6–2.8 per cent of GDP (ibid.: 21).

A putative reform would necessitate increasing employment rates by (apart from easing employment protection and cutting payroll taxes) eliminating easy access to early retirement schemes and disability benefits as well as raising farmers' social security contributions. That would doubtless produce a fierce backlash. Likewise, privatisation of state-owned companies (including railways and the national post), involving cost rationalisation and redundancies, would run counter to the interests of trade unions. Nevertheless, such reform programmes need to be embarked upon if prosperity in the urban centres and peripheral regions alike is to be forthcoming.

Furthermore, much needs to be done in the area of higher

education. As mentioned earlier, the ossified public education system – itself the legacy of communist times – that stifles internal competition and breeds academic mediocrity seems absolutely unsuited to the challenges of the information age (OECD, 2008). Public universities, often resembling change-averse bureaucracies, are run as 'fiefs' where innovations such as teaching by outside practitioners or introducing teamwork are resisted. Rote learning is still favoured, with little emphasis being placed on individual analysis and creative thinking. In sum, the Polish system could do much more to enable students to compete in a modern-day labour market, where an employee's greatest assets are flexibility, capacity to innovative and creativity.

In the same vein, a reprioritisation of public spending – that is, cutting down on expenditure on inefficient agriculture, loss-making industry and bloated administration – might allow both the government and businesses to increase investment in R&D, innovation and ICT deployment. Unless disproportionate amounts of taxpayers' money stop flowing to farmers, industry workers and civil servants, the country's knowledge-economy potential will suffer, which, in turn, will affect its competitiveness and longer-term development prospects. It is obviously a moot point whether or how much the government should spend on R&D, education and training. Such spending, however, at least has the potential to raise productivity. Spending regional development money on subsidising industries that are unable to be profitable in their own right, however, systematically keeps resources in low-productivity industries.

Regional development works best when there is strong social capital. Some authors have emphasised the role of 'social dialogue' (Gardawski, 2007; Jasiecki, 2007). An aspect of this, of course, is harmonious employment relations, which have under-pinned economic success in Ireland and Spain. What is needed is reciprocal trust and willingness to compromise. Yet Polish society, pervaded by the spirit of polarisation and mistrust, encouraged by communism, has considerable difficulty with dialogue and consensus-seeking. This view was partly borne out by a spectacular wave of union-led strikes and protests that swept through Poland in mid-2007 and at the beginning of 2008. To a wider public, this epitomised, on the one hand, the confronta-tional nature of Polish industrial relations and the government's inept handling of negotiations and, on the other, emphasised the necessity of reform. Management styles in Poland tend to give little room for the employee voice (Maczynski, 1994; Pańków and Gąciarz, 2006). This state of affairs is somewhat reminiscent of that in the UK in the 1980s, which was resolved by radical change to reduce the power of trade unions both in the workplace but also in the political and economic decision-making structures. Forcing through such liberalisation would call for a politician of a Thatcher-like calibre, with vision, courage and single-mindedness, and a big majority due to a split opposition. Unfortunately, the vast majority of Polish decision-makers are – ideologically and psychologically – the antithesis of Lady Thatcher. Indeed, the ruling coalition that won the parliamentary elections in 2007 is loath to take tough, unpopular but indispensable decisions, and has actually deferred free-market reform.

The merits of further decentralisation

Large-scale economic liberalisation would have to be accom-panied by further decentralisation. More power should be devolved from the centre to the regions so that voivodships can eliminate the barriers that prevent economic adjustment. This, in turn, would enable them to make optimal use of their local resources and comparative advantage and hence pursue their individual development agenda. Admittedly, this is of relevance to all regions – poorer and richer alike. But it is the fortunes of depressed (peripheral) voivodships as well as many disadvantaged subregions (even within the prosperous regions) which depend most on the progress of decentralisation and liberalisation.

Indeed, to less-favoured regions, decentralisation (together with liberalisation) would offer the opportunity to 'enliven' or 'reinvigorate' (non-functioning) local labour markets. Thus decentralisation must be far reaching and relate to regulation rather than just to public finance and administration. Regional authorities should be allowed to set their own minimum wage – or to abolish it for that matter – and to adjust social security contributions to local wages. The idea would be to allow regions to reflect differences in productivity and the cost of living so as to stem the process of pricing the less productive out of legal employment. This de facto regionalisation of payroll taxes and the minimum wage would facilitate the creation of badly needed jobs in lower-productivity service industries.

Decentralisation, entailing the devolution of power in the area of taxation, could also benefit poorer voivodships. They are usually discriminated against by foreign businesses, for which the regional differences in labour costs resulting from the lack of economic adjustment play a marginal role in location decisions. To multinationals, what really matters is well-developed infrastructure and highly skilled human resources, which are available in better-off regions. Why not allow regional authorities, then, to set their own corporate income tax rates, thereby fostering inter-regional competition? This would enable depressed and/or peripheral regions – potentially unattractive to foreign investors – to offset their inherent disadvantages and also create tax competition, which, of itself, can restrain the power of government. Such a proposal would not distort competition and could constitute a viable systemic solution.[1] In contrast, the aforesaid SEZs, which offer tax breaks and other investment incentives, are designated by Warsaw-based ministers on an arbitrary basis.

In this context, it is worth mentioning the Regional Innovation Strategies (RIS) programme, which was carried out in 2004–06 with a view to boosting the innovation potential of the voivodships. Specifically, the idea was to enhance the competitiveness of small and medium-sized enterprises through the introduction of new technologies, the upgrading of ICT skills and the reinforcement of links between businesses and universities. Each voivodship was supposed to prepare an RIS that laid out concrete, locally specific tasks to be undertaken in order to achieve the above-mentioned objectives. Even though the implementation of the programme left much to be desired, its actual rationale was problematic.

Such efforts, if not accompanied by decentralisation and liberalisation, are bound to be ineffective (Zientara, 2008b). The belief

---

1   This is also important because of the co-financing character of EU regional aid. Since Brussels co-funds initiatives proposed by local authorities in Regional Development Strategies, richer voivodships might potentially be able to earmark more financial resources for the co-financing and, as a result, to implement more (bigger-scale) projects. In consequence, with rebuilt infrastructure and upgraded human resources, there is a risk that well-developed regions will become even more attractive to investment, which might foster further regional disproportions.

Table 12 Total EU regional aid for Polish regions (2004–13)

	May 2004–June 2006 (3.4 zlotys = 1€)			EU financial resources available for Polish regions in 2007–13	
	EU contribution to all projects (billion zlotys)	Number of implemented projects	EU contribution per capita (zlotys)	In absolute terms (billion euro)	Per capita (euro)
Dolnośląskie	4.9	2,537	1,695	1.6	554
Kujawsko-pomorskie	2.1	4,016	996	1.2	580
Lubelskie	1.6	5,474	724	1.5	688
Lubuskie	0.8	1,148	842	0.6	595
Łódzkie	2.0	4,290	763	1.2	466
Małopolskie	2.6	3,711	785	1.6	490
Mazowieckie	9.0	7,866	1,731	2.5	485
Opolskie	0.9	1,771	860	0.6	573
Podkarpackie	1.5	2,460	724	1.5	715
Podlaskie	0.9	4,190	744	0.8	667
Pomorskie	4.4	3,882	2,018	1.2	546
Śląskie (Silesia)	5.6	3,075	1,187	2.1	448
Świętokrzyskie	1.0	3,216	763	1.0	778
Warmińsko-mazurskie	2.8	2,566	1,990	1.3	910
Wielkopolskie	3.7	6,280	1,091	1.6	474
Zachodniopomorskie	3.0	2,836	1,823	1.1	649

Source: Author's calculations based on the data provided by the Ministry of Regional Development; available at: www.mrr.gov.pl/

that such undertakings per se may resolve the problems of Polish regions seems to be unrealistic and naive. It comes across as just another illustration of the activism of technocrats and politicians, who tend to devise such fine-sounding theoretical strategies, at the same time doing virtually nothing to allow them to produce really tangible results. Such a stance typifies the unwillingness of decision-makers to cope with more intractable problems: it is much easier to announce the creation of an otherwise sensible and uncontroversial programme than to press on with unpopular but necessary reforms.

Other activist measures, such as the establishment by regional authorities of science and technology parks or so-called entrepreneurship 'incubators' (see also Matusiak, 2003), where people setting up small businesses can benefit from assorted support (free consulting, free access to ICT, free rent, etc.), might be useful, but their effectiveness is open to doubt. Newly born entrepreneurs are still burdened with centre-imposed excessive bureaucracy and high payroll taxes. Again, such undertakings, if not accompanied by decentralisation and liberalisation, will be far less effective. This confirms our conviction that what Polish regions urgently need is a sort of eclectic strategy, combining free-market reform with certain premises of the new regionalism.

It follows that various measures taken by regional authorities with a view to promoting self-employment and technological advancement – but uncoordinated with structural change and power devolution – are unlikely to unfetter entrepreneurial dynamism. That the Polish have business acumen and a German-like work ethic is borne out by the spectacular small-business boom in 1989–93 – when economic freedom was still relatively unrestrained and the country was deservedly regarded as a 'tiger' of eastern Europe – and the generally excellent reputation Polish workers have recently earned in the UK, Ireland and elsewhere in the EU. The next section demonstrates the nature and dynamics of change.

The process of change

We will now look at the mechanism of coordination of economic liberalisation and institutional decentralisation with the use of the Structural Funds and the application of some new-regionalism concepts, focusing on concrete examples. Before moving on, however, it might be informative to have a look at the volume of regional support earmarked for Poland. In absolute terms, Poland is the biggest beneficiary of EU aid among the new member states. In 2007–13, the country will receive in total €67.3 billion from the Structural Funds and the Cohesion Fund, of which one third will be managed by regional authorities (Table 12).

Regional transport initiatives

As noted above, one of the main characteristics of Polish region-alism is that it is within regions themselves that the socio-economic differences are most conspicuous. While in large urban areas unemployment may well be as low as 3–4 per cent, in many subregions situated in the same voivodship it might easily top 15 per cent. This means that it is in big and medium-sized cities that jobs are mainly generated and intra-regional labour mobility – that is, commuting from the local periphery to the urban areas (50–60 kilometres one way) – should be facilitated.

In Poland, the railways function as a primary means of

transport. Yet the Polish railway company (PKP) is a state-owned monopolist dominated by trade unions that successfully block downsizing and rationalisation. In voivodships railway services are provided by the PKP regional companies (so-called *Przewozy regionalne*). Predictably, as strong unions thwart restructuring efforts, the quality of services is low and the tickets are expensive, which is very important given low disposable incomes in the most disadvantaged subregions. Usually, local authorities have a minority stake in these companies though in practice they are unable to influence their policy.

This should be changed. First, deregulation of the railways – through letting in other (private-owned foreign and/or national) providers of railway services – would intensify competition. To achieve that, union opposition would also have to be overcome, hence the need to reduce union power, which is an important facet of free-market reform. More competition would generally mean lower prices and better quality of service. The appropriate mechanism to fund railways in a free-market economy is a matter of some debate.[2] Nevertheless, arguably a productive use of available EU money would be a sorely needed modernisation of railway infrastructure.[3] Similar points can be made regarding the need to modernise the road system and airport infrastructure.[4]

---

2   Some economists would argue for fully private finance, others have argued for a levy on land values (or on businesses benefiting from infrastructure), still others argue that, because of the low marginal cost of railway travel, there has to be some government involvement in infrastructure finance.

3   Again, it is a matter of debate to what extent regional aid from the EU should be provided. But, given that it is provided, the renewal of infrastructure is one of the more productive ways to use it.

4   In 2006 in Warmińsko-mazurskie region there were 815 deaths per 1 million passengers, one of the highest ratios in the entire EU. In the region of Bremen, for the sake of comparison, there were only 23 deaths per 1 million passengers.

Once again, though, we see the link between regional policy and the need for labour market and business liberalisation. Many of the poor regions are potentially attractive for tourism and relatively low costs should allow tourism and related industries to flourish. Better infrastructure would be helpful in promoting tourism. Unless, however, there are conditions in which business can flourish and employ labour at pay rates justified by an employee's productivity, then such service industries will not develop.

The role of EU regional aid

By Western standards, the magnitude of infrastructure neglect is enormous. Without EU regional subsidies, it will be practically impossible to build and/or renovate roads, railway tracks, edifices or treatment plants in the foreseeable future. We do not debate the long-term merits of EU regional aid here, nor whether the aid programme is beneficial for the EU as a whole. Regional aid used in an appropriate way is, however, an important ingredient if regional development is going to happen quickly in the new EU countries. Whereas Polish big cities (and in particular their centres) do not differ much from their western European counterparts, small provincial towns and villages still look as if communism had not ended. And this holds true not only for poor rural regions situated in the east, but also for many subregions located in the more prosperous west and centre.

Arguably, such regional disparities and, especially, intra-regional contrasts are typical of the whole of central and eastern Europe (with the possible exception of Slovenia). All the capital regions – with higher-than-average GDP per capita and high levels of foreign direct investment – are vibrant with economic activity.

By contrast, in Lithuanian or Romanian remote rural regions, the situation is even worse than in their Polish counterparts. Across central and eastern Europe the periphery has borne the brunt of communist mismanagement and post-communist neglect.

Thus there is a need to make optimal use of EU regional subsidies. Where regional aid is provided it should be used in a way that allows regions to make best use of their comparative advantages. Depressed areas do not have to become milieus of innovation. They should be allowed to focus on job creation in lower-end services such as tourism and higher-value-added farming. Big cities and more prosperous regions, by contrast, may well have a comparative advantage in ICT and related industries which rely on continual innovation.

What is necessary is a combination of national-level liberalisation (which should be supported, where relevant, by liberalisation at the EU level too) and decentralisation to enable regions to develop policies that allow them to exploit their comparative advantage. Government intervention and regional policy should be of the form that is likely to be benign, at worst, promoting infrastructure development, ICT deployment and HR upgrading. Innovation, the development of social capital and adaptation in the context of a free-enterprise society will also be vital for regional development. The evidence from Silesia suggests that this is possible.

Silesia: towards the learning region

Śląskie voivodship or, to be more precise, its subregion of Upper Silesia is a traditional old industrial region that is in the process of turning itself around. Compared with other Polish regions, it

Box 3 Śląskie (Silesia): a historical background

For centuries, Silesia was not part of Poland, being either a quasi-independent principality or a province governed by the Czechs or the Austrian Habsburgs. In 1742 it was annexed by Prussia. In 1922, as a result of the plebiscites commissioned by the League of Nations, the eastern part of Upper Silesia (a subregion of Silesia) was incorporated into Poland. Only after World War II did the whole of Silesia find itself within the boundaries of the country. All this affected the region's development and its relationship with the rest of Poland. In the eighteenth and nineteenth centuries Upper Silesia, in contrast to most Polish territories, experienced the Industrial Revolution. Coal mining and heavy industry stimulated economic growth and intensive urbanisation, which, in turn, made Upper Silesia reminiscent of typical coal districts in the UK. The region was as technologically advanced and dynamically entrepreneurial. Industrial activity was so intense and labour in such demand that migrants, especially from the territories under Russian and Austrian rule, arrived, causing cities to grow. Once within the confines of Poland after the end of World War II, Upper Silesia stood out from the rest of the country owing to a long history of separation from the Polish state and a different pattern of socio-economic development, a non-standard language, the presence of a considerable German minority, strong social bonds and a distinctive work ethic. Those differences persisted – notwithstanding the communists' attempts to eradicate them – only to resurface with intensity after 1989, when a few local activists voiced separatist demands in reaction to a growing sense of despair stemming from the decline of the coal industry and the hardships of the transformation. Under communism, Upper Silesia's mines and steel works became a driving force behind the country's industrialisation. Unsurprisingly, the authorities perceived Upper Silesia as a national treasure, while the miner toiling down the pit was put on the communist pedestal. Hence political patronage and exceptional privileges were lavished on miners and on the region. Roads and hospitals were built there and miners could buy products unavailable in the rest of Poland in special shops.

is atypical in many respects (see Box 3). The entire area is highly urbanised and marked by the concentration of heavy industry (including the state-owned coal-mining sector, which has for years generated huge financial losses). Overall, there are seventeen comparatively large cities in Upper Silesia, whose boundaries touch each other. Of course, typical woes affecting such regions, such as air pollution, industrial dereliction, landscape devastation and environmental degradation, still affect the quality of life. Socioculturally, the region also stands out: a German-like work ethic coupled with the strong social bonds and spirit of solidarity that characterise communities where – owing to dangerous conditions of work – trust and cooperation play a pivotal role. All this explains the comparatively high quality of Silesian social capital.

When communism came to an end and triggered the closure of several state-owned enterprises, the region found itself on the brink of a precipice. There was an urgent need to turn it around. And, as things stood in 2008, it is fair to say that the region has managed to capitalise on its strengths and – notwithstanding the unresolved question of the mining industry – has asserted its prominent position among Poland's regions, on a par with the capital region of Mazowieckie (Table 8).

In the event, the entire region has an inherent edge over other Polish areas. These include: (i) geographical proximity to Germany and the Czech Republic; (ii) well-developed road and ICT infrastructure; (iii) a highly-skilled workforce; (iv) a comparatively large number of universities and R&D institutes (Table 9); and, crucially, (v) high levels of social capital. All this somehow helps to outweigh the relatively lower quality of life stemming from mining-induced environmental degradation and industrial dereliction.

Critically, Silesia has managed to take full advantage of globalisation and EU integration, successfully attracting FDI. The region has an automotive industry and advanced-engineering cluster. From 1989 to 2004 the car industry invested $4 billion in the area. It is also notable that 54 out of Poland's biggest national and foreign-owned firms (many of them are in the high-tech sector) are situated in Silesia, whose share of the country's total FDI amounts to 14.4 per cent. Only the capital region of Mazowieckie scores better on that count.

Compromise-building, partnership and cooperation have been important ingredients of growth. Take, for instance, the Siemianowice Employment Pact (a grassroots, bottom-up initiative and the first of its kind in the whole country), which is aimed at fighting unemployment in the voivodship (Zientara, 2008b). It is modelled on the Dublin Employment Pact and was built around the partnership between local job centres, city mayors and councillors, church officials (with the archbishop of Silesia to the fore), craftsmen's guilds, trade unions and private businesses. The initiative, albeit formally signed by all the actors, has no trappings of a typical bureaucratic institution. It simply promoted openness, flexibility and creativity. This pact is a genuine novelty in Poland but has been important in rebuilding social capital.

In a similar vein, plans are currently afoot to set up a huge conurbation consisting of the region's seventeen biggest cities. The city mayors have voluntarily agreed to implement this. In effect, they form a federation with power being distributed by bottom-up agreement and not by top-down diktat. The initiative could be regarded as an example of 'interlocal co-operative agreements that generate collective benefit by producing efficiencies and economies of scale in the provision and production of services and by internalising spillover problems' (Feiock, 2007: 49). In this sense, the plan in its conceptualisation touches upon the issue of – to use Feiock's term – institutional collective action (ICA), deeply rooted in 'second-generation' rational choice models (Ostrom, 2005). ICA refers to the mechanisms – decentralised voluntary governance arrangements – by which 'two or more governments act collectively to capture the gains from providing or producing services across a larger area' (Feiock, 2007: 48).

The Silesian authorities believe that a metropolis of that stature – apart from providing efficiencies and savings – could possibly enter the top tier of the European urban hierarchy. In this way, one can see the process of institutional learning, innovation and adaptation to new circumstances resulting from bottom-up cooperation, albeit at governmental level.

11 CONCLUSION

In this monograph, we have focused predominantly on Poland, while analysing regional differences within the EU and the effectiveness of regional aid. We have examined the relationship between a country's nationwide business climate and the attractiveness of its regions as well as highlighted the merits of certain aspects of the new regionalism together with the concept of the learning region. In principle, Poland – despite being bigger and having a complicated history – is not much different from other recent EU entrants and can serve as an illustration of regional problems. The policy approach we have proposed is not intended to be Polish-specific but general in character and hence applicable to other European countries. That is why the emphasis is placed upon a combination of nationwide liberalisation and decentralisation with the appropriate use of EU regional aid and the application of some new-regionalism prescriptions.

Yet we should also consider issues of far broader scope. These concern the underlying strengths and weaknesses of the EU's economic model and the challenges brought forth by enlargement and globalisation, as well as the political ramifications of European regionalism for the standing of national governments and, ultimately, the future modus operandi of an EU of 27 or more. We believe that the regional perspective has provided a number of informative insights. The EU as a whole and – to varying degrees

– its individual member states need more economic and political freedom as well as the recognition of the necessity of change if the process of economic development is to exist. This holds true especially for countries such as Poland – a new poor entrant that has been outclassed in the area of free-market reform by its central and eastern European neighbours.

All this has affected the situation in Poland's most disadvantaged regions. With liberalisation and decentralisation stalled, these voivodships – being deprived of adequate instruments to pursue their development strategies – might have considerable difficulty in catching up not only with their richer counterparts in the West, but also in central and eastern Europe. The current institutional arrangements make it difficult for depressed regions to make best use of their potential. Thus economic and political reform is needed both at EU and member state level.

New entrants from central and eastern Europe, rather than copying the Western social model, should press ahead with economic liberalisation, thereby providing a powerful incentive for change in Old Europe. EU-15 countries, in turn, ought to liberalise their economies far more rapidly. This is particularly relevant given the rise of China and India as well as the underlying strengths of the USA. Liberalisation of labour markets should be given top priority. Compared with the USA, Europe's average unemployment rates are still high and joblessness rates in many regions are of the order of 15 per cent. EU regional aid designed both to requalify the unemployed and to build/renovate infrastructure is bound to be ineffectual unless it is accompanied by deep structural change. The experience of East Germany clearly demonstrates this.

It is encouraging that many central and eastern European

countries (the Baltic republics, Romania, Slovakia, but also Macedonia and Bosnia), in sharp contrast to Poland, have decided to press on with free-market reform. Although one can detect clear symptoms of reform fatigue – witness the electoral victories of populist parties in Slovakia and Lithuania which promise to end 'inhumane neo-liberal experiments' – those countries should not change course and settle for a watered-down version of Old Europe-style welfarism.

Judging by the results of the reformist efforts in Ireland and Spain, this drive for liberalisation, coupled with appropriate regional policy, can help reduce the development gap between regions. Of course, it is the capital regions which are bound to catch up fastest. Yet the fruits of rapid economic growth are likely to lift living standards in most depressed regions, too. That is why the accession process might be seen as an injection of fresh blood, giving momentum to necessary reform. But, in the eyes of an increasingly large number of EU-15 citizens, the most visible consequences of enlargement are not lower prices of goods and services, but what some regard as the 'stealing' of jobs as a result of 'unfair' competition. All this risks producing a backlash against integration in general and further enlargement in particular, as exemplified by the rejection of the European constitution by French and Dutch voters. Hence, with doubts being cast over the EU's *raison d'être*, one can discern enlargement fatigue both in Brussels and many EU-15 capitals.

Crucially, this state of affairs has led some high-ranking politicians and officials alike to rekindle the debate on the merits (and shortcomings) of a 'two-speed' or, more generally, 'multi-speed' Europe. So the notions and mechanisms of differentiated integration – as implied by the very idea of multi-speed Europe

– have become the subject of much controversy. The Lisbon Treaty – which, despite the Irish rejection, might eventually come into force – is not in principle consonant with the concept of differentiated integration. The treaty, seen by its proponents as a *sine qua non* condition of the Community's more efficient functioning, comes across as a uniformity-imposing endeavour. By contrast, the idea of a multi-speed Europe suggests that 'some countries could push ahead, others could hold back and the union as a whole would evolve from a monolithic one-size-fits-all block into a club in which membership would mean different things to different people' (Economist, 2007b: 34).

So the idea of a multi-speed Europe might ease the tensions resulting from countries' differing attitudes towards integration and, at the same time, lay the foundations of a new modus operandi. In practice, it could possibly take one of two basic forms. The first type – variously described as 'core Europe', 'concentric circles' or 'two-speed Europe' – would entail creating an inner circle of countries determined to press ahead with integration in all areas; they would constitute a sort of club within the club. The other members, forming the outer ring, would cooperate only on selected issues. In the second type – called 'coalitions of the willing', 'enhanced cooperation' or 'variable geometry' – all countries would agree to abide by a basic set of rules (most probably, the common market). Then smaller groups would voluntarily cooperate in particular areas (say, foreign affairs or immigration policy). In fact, there could be many such groupings with overlapping memberships (all countries would simultaneously belong to different groups according to their interests).

The latter concept seems to offer an interesting and plausible alternative. Its undeniable merit is that it actually works. Suffice

Box 4 Eastern European countries and early euro membership

On 1 January 2007 Slovenia became the first ex-communist state to enter the euro zone. On 1 January 2009 Slovakia also did so. Whereas for such small and open economies as Slovenia, Slovakia or Estonia the advantages of entering the euro zone are likely to outweigh the drawbacks, for big open economies such as those of Poland and Hungary, the adoption of the euro in the near future will be less beneficial than many economists believe. To simplify, the adoption of the euro involves the loss of an independent monetary policy. This means that the European Central Bank will set the interest rates both for well-developed Old Europe economies, which grow slower, and for poorer New Europe ones, which grow faster. A single monetary policy is inappropriate for such a diverse group: the fast-developing countries of eastern Europe may require higher interests rates, while the EU-15 requires lower rates. If lower rates are adopted in new European countries then the resulting accommodation would have to be facilitated by fiscal policy, wage flexibility and enhanced labour mobility. Yet all eastern Euro-candidates have – to varying degrees – difficulty implementing such policies. That said, in smaller open economies (such as those of Latvia, Estonia and Lithuania), the benefits of early euro membership stemming from greater stability and market liquidity as well as increased trade may outweigh its negative consequences. In bigger economies (such as those of Poland, Hungary and the Czech Republic) – where, indeed, the governments struggle with budget deficits and wage flexibility is relatively low – early entry into the euro area, coupled with the Balassa-Samuelson effect, risks producing, among much else, serious problems with high inflation.* We must also remember that one of the essential preconditions for the proper functioning of the optimal currency zone is a substantial degree of *real* convergence between member countries. Needless to say, none of the would-be candidates for euro membership from eastern Europe meets this prerequisite. The financial crisis and the sudden depreciation of the zloty in October 2008, however – in sharp contrast to the Slovakian krona – highlighted the significant advantage of euro membership (safe haven). As a result, the government declared that it would like Poland to adopt the euro in 2012.

Source: Zientara (2006b: 3–10)
*For discussion, see Grauwe and Schnabl (2004) and Zientara (2006b).

it to say that, out of 27 countries, fifteen have so far adopted the euro (see Box 4), de facto forming a coalition of the willing to cooperate in the area of monetary policy, and that fifteen countries (including three non-EU states) signed up to the Schengen agreement, thereby collaborating in the (narrow) area of the passport-free flow of people. In this way the idea of 'variable geometry' could enable countries interested in closer integration in specific (and often controversial) domains to move ahead without pressurising those who simply want to stand by.

This would not only lead to an EU that was more democratic and pluralistic, but would also eliminate the potential source of intra-EU friction and might simultaneously pave the ground for the accession of such contentious candidates as Turkey. It follows that, with a higher degree of heterogeneity, the idea of 'coalitions of the willing' lends itself far better to constituting the fundamental guiding principle of an enlarged EU than the above-mentioned concept of 'core Europe'. The latter would automatically produce a sharp dividing line between two groups of countries, whereby members of the group moved at the same pace as each other and the groups as a whole moved at different paces.

The adoption of the 'coalition of the willing' model would be in the interests of most new member states. They might more easily deflect the pressure applied by French or German politicians to harmonise labour legislation, tax rates and welfare benefits. In this context, it has to be remembered that, as mentioned in Chapter 3, would-be members such as Macedonia or Bosnia have already introduced even lower (flat) taxes and cut red tape more radically than, say, Estonia or Latvia, and, therefore, are likely to be more attractive to investors than most existing EU countries. Transplanting a Western-style welfare state into central and eastern Europe (as the case of East Germany exemplifies) would be a step in the wrong direction, though this does not have to rule out benign government involvement in promoting ICT and innovation generation, as in the case of Estonia.

It seems that both new and would-be member states as well as the entire EU might be better off if the 'coalitions of the willing' approach was pursued.[1] Of course, there would also be some implications for regional policy. A looser-knit union – whose (richer) members might naturally feel less obliged to support pan-European cohesion with their money – could mean less regional

---

1   Possibly, the CAP might then be thoroughly overhauled, with those countries keen to subsidise and protect their farmers doing so with their own taxpayers' money.

aid for the EU-12. Arguably, this issue would be thrown into even sharper focus if the 'two-speed' Europe model were to be adopted (the members of the inner core would undoubtedly suggest to poorer countries from the outer ring that, if they wanted financial support, they would have to be consistent and integrate more). Nonetheless, one can reasonably expect that the European Commission – determined to reduce regional disparities – would apply pressure on the affluent and play a decisive role in reconciling the conflicting attitudes.

The 'coalitions of the willing' model would smooth the path for further enlargement to the south and, with reservations, to the east (for example, to include Ukraine). If the existing modus operandi is not modified, the accession of new poorer countries from southern Europe is likely to intensify the tensions along the hypothetical division line between the potential core, which is overtly hostile towards Turkish membership and sceptical about Albania's or Macedonia's membership, and an informal alliance between the UK, Ireland and some central and eastern European members (Poland, Romania, the Baltic republics), which are generally willing to admit all Balkan states. The resulting escalation of intra-EU friction and the possible standstill would be counterproductive and harmful to all the parties.

EU decision-makers ought to realise that expanding the scope of economic and political freedom is the best way of addressing the EU's internal problems. Contrary to the popular belief, still held by the proponents of 'core Europe', it is not harmonisation-driven uniformity and narrow-minded exclusionism but diversity and openness which would enhance the Community's dynamism and strength. And, having experienced such a reinvention, a more liberal, more loosely knit Union will be conducive to improving the wellbeing of the citizens of new and old members alike. The former will be given the real opportunity to bridge the development gap, and the latter the opportunity to capitalise on the benefits offered by the processes of European and global integration.

REFERENCES

Abraham, F. and P. Van Rompuy (1995), 'Regional convergence in the European Monetary Union', *Papers in Regional Science*, 74(2): 125–42.

Amabile, T. M., R. Conti, H. Coon, J. Lazenby and M. Herron (1996), 'Assessing the work environment for creativity', *Academy of Management Journal*, 39(5): 1154–84.

Amin, N. and N. Thrift (2002), *Cities: Reimagining the Urban*, Cambridge: Polity Press.

Anselin, L., A. Varga and Z. J. Acs (1997), 'Local geographical spillovers between university research and high technology innovations', *Journal of Urban Economics*, 42(3): 422–48.

Appadurai, A. (1996), *Modernity at Large: Cultural Dimensions of Globalization*, Minneapolis: University of Minnesota Press.

Armstrong, H. and J. Taylor (2000), *Regional Economics and Policy*, Oxford: Blackwell.

Arrow, K. J. (1962), 'Economic welfare and the allocation of resources for invention', in R. R. Nielsen (ed.), *The Rate and Direction of Inventive Activity*, Princeton, NJ: Princeton University Press, pp. 609–25.

Asheim, B. (1996), 'Industrial districts as "learning regions": a condition for prosperity', *European Planning Studies*, 4(4): 379–400.

Bafoil, F. (1999) 'Post-communist borders and territories. Conflicts, learning and rule building in Poland', *International Journal of Urban and Regional Research*, 23(3): 567–82.

Balcerowicz, L. (2003), *Toward the Limited State*, Washington, DC: World Bank.

Balcerowicz, L., B. Błaszczyk and M. Dąbrowskim (1997), 'The Polish way to the market economy 1989–1995', in S. Parker, J. D. Sachs and W. T. Woo (eds), *Economies in Transition*, Cambridge, MA: MIT Press, pp. 131–60.

Barro, R. J. and X. Sala-I-Martin (1995), *Economic Growth*, New York: McGraw-Hill.

Beddoes, Z. M. (2008), 'When fortune frowned', *The Economist*, 8601, 11 October, pp. 3–34.

Begg, I. (2008), 'Cohesion in the EU', CESifo Forum 1/2008, 3–9; available at: www.cesifo-group.de/.

BISER (2002), 'E-Europe Regions – Development Model. Deliverable 3 of the BISER Project', Information Society Technology Programme, IST-2000–30187.

Boekema, F., K. Morgan, S. Bakkers and R. Rutten (2000), 'Introduction to learning regions; a new issue for analysis', in F. Boekema, K. Morgan, S. Bakkers and R. Rutten (eds), *Knowledge, Innovation and Economic Growth: The Theory and Practice of Learning Regions*, Cheltenham: Edward Elgar, pp. 3–16.

Boschma, R. (2005), 'Proximity and innovation. A critical assessment', *Regional Studies*, 39(1): 61–74.

Botero, J., S. Djankov, R. La Porta, F. Lopez-de-Silanes and A. Shleifer (2004), 'The regulation of labor', *Quarterly Journal of Economics*, 119: 1339–82; website dataset available at: www.economics.harvard.edu/faculty/shleifer/shleifer.html/.

Bradley, J., G. Untiedt and T. Mitze (2007), *Analysis of the Impact of Cohesion Policy: A Note Explaining the HERMIN-based Simulations*; available at: http://ec.europa.eu/regional_policy/sources/docgener/evaluation/pdf/hermin07.pdf/.

Brakman, S. and H. Garretsen (2005), *Location and Competition*, New York: Routledge.

Brenner, N. (1998), 'Global cities, glocal states: global city formation and state territorial restructuring in contemporary Europe', *Review of International Political Economy*, 5(1): 1–37.

Brenner, N. (1999), 'Globalization as reterritorialization: the re-scaling of urban governance in Europe', *Urban Studies*, 36(3): 431–51.

Brenner, N. (2004), *New State Spaces: Urban Governance and the Rescaling of Statehood*, Oxford: Oxford University Press.

Breschi, S. and F. Lissoni (2001), 'Localised knowledge spillovers vs. innovative milieux: knowledge "tacitness" reconsidered', *Papers in Regional Science*, 80(3): 255–73.

Breschi, S. and F. Malerba (eds) (2005), *Clusters, Networks and Innovation*, Oxford: Oxford University Press.

Bush, V. (1945), *Science: The Endless Frontier*, Washington, DC: United States Government Printing Office.

Carlsson, B. and R. Stankiewicz (1991), 'On the nature, function and composition of innovation systems', *Journal of Evolutionary Economics*, 1(2): 93–118.

Carson, I. (2007), 'Who are the champions', *The Economist*, 8515, 10 February, pp. 3–14.

Castells, M. (1996), *The Rise of the Network Society*, Oxford: Blackwell.

Castells, M. (2001), *The Internet Galaxy – Reflections on the Internet, Business and Society*, New York and Oxford: Oxford University Press.

Castro, E. A. and C. N. Jensen-Butler (1991), *Flexibility and the Neo-classical Model in the Analysis of Regional Growth*, Aarhus: Institute of Political Science, University of Aarhus.

Castro, E. A. and C. N. Jensen-Butler (2003), 'Demand for innovation and communication technology-based services and regional economic development', *Papers in Regional Science*, 82(1): 27–50.

Chaplin, H., M. Gorton and S. Davidova (2007), 'Impediments to the diversification of rural economies in central and eastern Europe: evidence from small-scale farms in Poland', *Regional Studies*, 41(3): 361–76.

Chen, M.-H. and G. Kaufman (2008), 'Employee creativity and R&D: a critical review', *Creativity and Innovation Management*, 17(1): 71–6.

Clark, M. (2001) *Teleworking in the Countryside: Home-based Working in the Information Society*, Aldershot: Ashgate.

Coleman, J. (1988), 'Social capital in the creation of human capital', *American Journal of Sociology*, 94: 95–120.

Cooke, P. (ed.) (1995), *The Rise of the Rustbelt*, London: UCL Press.

Cooke, P. and K. Morgan (1998), *The Associational Economy: Firms, Regions and Innovation*, Oxford: Oxford University Press.

Cornford, C., A. Gillespie and R. Richardson (1996), 'Regional development in the information society: a review and analysis', Paper prepared for the EU High Level Expert Group on the Social and Societal Aspects of Information Society, CURDS, University of Newcastle.

Cottrell, R. (2003), 'When East Meets West', *The Economist*, 8351, 22 November, pp. 3–20.

Cox, K. R. (1998), 'Spaces of dependence, spaces of engagement and the politics of scale, or: looking for local politics', *Political Geography*, 17(1): 1–23.

Cox, K. R. (2005), 'The global and the local', in P. Cloke and R. J. Johnston (eds), *Human Geography's Binaries*, London: Sage, pp. 175–99.

Cumbers, A. and D. MacKinnon (2005), *Clusters in Urban and Regional Development*, London: Routledge.

Davies, N. (1996), *Europe: A History*, Oxford: Oxford University Press.

Davis, M. (1998), *Ecology of Fear: Los Angeles and the Imagination of Disaster*, New York: Metropolitan Books.

Decker, F. (2002), 'Governance beyond the nation-state: reflections on the democratic deficit of the European Union', *Journal of European Public Policy*, 9(2): 256–72.

DeFilipis, J. (2004), *Unmaking Goliath: Community Control in the Face of Global Capital*, New York: Routledge.

De Michelis, N. (2008), 'Regional convergence: a relevant measure of policy success?', CESifo Forum 1/2008, 10–13; available at: www.cesifo-group.de/.

Dolfsma, W. (2008), *Knowledge Economies. Organization, Location and Innovation*, London and New York: Routledge.

Dreier, P. J., J. H. Mollenkopf and T. Swanstrom (2001), *Place Matters: Metropolitics for the Twenty-first Century*, Lawrence: University Press of Kansas.

Economist (2001), 'Jobs, please', *The Economist*, 8224, 31 March, p. 33.

Economist (2006a), 'Not yet free to serve', *The Economist*, 8465, 18
    February, p. 28.

Economist (2006b), 'Ducking change, the European way', *The
    Economist*, 8474, 22 April, p. 32.

Economist (2007a), 'Rich man, poor man', *The Economist*, 8512,
    20 January, p. 12.

Economist (2007b), 'Coalitions for the willing', *The Economist*,
    8514, 3 February, p. 34.

Economist (2008), 'Under the threat of change', *The Economist*,
    8583, 7 June, pp. 35–6.

Ederveen, S. and J. Pelkmans (2006), 'Principles of subsidiarity',
    CPB Netherlands Bureau of Economic Policy.

Ederveen, S., H. L. F. de Groot and R. Nahuis (2006), 'Fertile soil
    for Structural Funds? A panel data analysis of the conditional
    effectiveness of European Cohesion Policy', *Kyklos*, 59: 17–42.

Esposti, R. (2008), 'Regional growth convergence and EU policies:
    empirical evidence and measuring problems', CESifo Forum
    1/2008, 14–22; available at: www.cesifo-group.de/.

Etzkowitz, H. (2001), 'The second academic revolution and the
    rise of entrepreneurial science', *Technology and Society*, 20(2):
    18–29.

European Central Bank (2004), 'Financial FDI to the EU
    Accession Countries', 19 March, Frankfurt.

European Commission (1998), 'Guidelines on National Regional
    Aid for 2000–2006', *Official Journal of the European Union*,
    C74, 10 March, Brussels.

European Commission (2006), 'Guidelines on National Regional
    Aid for 2007–2013', *Official Journal of the European Union*,
    C54, 4 March, Brussels.

European Commission (2007a), *Cohesion for Growth and Employment*, Luxembourg: OOPEC; available at: http://ec.europa.eu/financial_perspective/cohesion/.

European Commission (2007b), *Growing Regions, Growing Europe: Fourth Report on Economic and Social Cohesion*, Luxembourg: OOPEC.

European Commission (2007c), *Innovation Clusters in Europe: A Statistical Analysis and Overview of Current Policy Support, DG Enterprise and Industry Report*, Luxembourg: OOPEC; available at: www.europe-innova.org/index.jsp?type=page&cid=8702&lg=en/.

European Council (2006), 'Council Decision of 6 October 2006 on Community Strategic Guidelines on Cohesion' [2006/702/EC], *Official Journal of the European Union*, L291/11, 21 October.

Eurostat (2006), *Regions: Statistical Yearbook 2006*; available at: http://epp.eurostat.ec.europa.eu/.

Eurostat (2007), *Regions: Statistical Yearbook 2006*; available at: http://epp.eurostat.ec.europa.eu/.

Eurostat (2008), *Population and Social Conditions*; available at: http://epp.eurostat.ec.europa.eu/.

Falk, R. (2000), 'The decline of citizenship in an era of globalization', *Citizenship Studies*, 4(1): 5–18.

Featherstone, D. J. (2003), 'Spatialities of trans-national resistance to globalization: the maps of grievance of the inter-continental caravan', *Transactions of the Institute of British Geographers*, 28(4): 404–21.

Feiock, R. C. (2007), 'Rational choice and regional governance', *Journal of Urban Affairs*, 29(1): 47–63.

Feldman, M. P., J. Francis and J. Bercovitz (2005), 'Creating a cluster while building a firm: entrepreneurs and the formation of industrial clusters', *Regional Studies*, 39(1): 129–41.

Field, J. (2003), *Social Capital*, London: Routledge.

Florida, R. (2004), 'America's looming creativity crisis', *Harvard Business Review*, 82(10): 122–31.

Forbes (2005), *Network Readiness Index*; available at: www.forbes.com/2005/03/09/cx_0309wefranking.html/.

Fritsch, M. and C. Schwirten (1999), 'Enterprise–university co-operation and the role of public research institutions in regional innovation systems', *Industry and Innovation*, 6(1): 69–83.

Funck, B. and L. Pizzati (eds) (2003), *European Integration, Regional Policy, and Growth*, Washington, DC: World Bank.

García, R. and R. Calantone (2001), 'A critical look at technological innovation typology and innovativeness terminology: a literature review', *Journal of Product Innovation Management*, 19(2): 110–32.

Gardawski, J. (2007), 'Social dialogue from guild rights to the directives of the European Union', *Dialogue*, December, pp. 13–23.

Gelauff, G. and M. Pomp (2000), 'Deregulation and labour market reforms: the role of the social partners', in G. Galli and J. Pelkmans (eds), *Regulatory Reform and Competitiveness in Europe*, Cheltenham: Edward Elgar, pp. 381–429.

Gill, S. (1996), 'Globalization, democratization and the politics of indifference', in J. Mittelman (ed.), *Globalization: Critical Reflections*, Boulder, CO: Lynne Rienner, pp. 205–28.

Gillespie, A., R. Richardson and J. Comford (2001), 'Regional development and the new economy', Paper presented at the EIB conference, Luxembourg, January.

Goodhart, M. (2001), 'Democracy, globalization and the problem of the state', *Polity*, 33(4): 527–46.

Grabowska, M. and T. Szawiel (2001), *Building Democracy. Social Divisions, Political Parties and Civil Society in Post-Communist Poland*, Warsaw: PWN.

Graham, S. and S. Marvin (2001), *Telecommunications and the City: Electronic Spaces, Urban Places*, London: Routledge.

Grauwe, P. and G. Schnabl (2004), 'EMU strategies for the new member states', *Intereconomics, Review of European Economic Policy*, 39(5): 241–7.

Grosse, T. G. (2006), 'The East European quality of dialogue', *Dialogue*, June, pp. 23–30.

Harvey, D. (2006), *Spaces of Global Capitalism*, New York: Verso.

Hayek, F. A. von (1960), *The Constitution of Liberty*, Chicago, IL: University of Chicago Press.

Heritage Foundation (2008), *Index of Economic Freedom 2007*; available at: www.heritage.org/index/countries.cfm/.

Holston, J. (1999), 'Spaces of insurgent citizenship', in J. Holston (ed.), *Cities and Citizenship*, Durham, NC: Duke University Press, pp. 155–73.

Hryniewicz, J. (2007), 'Economic, political and cultural factors of space differentiation', *Przegląd Zachodni*, 2: 21–46.

Hudson, R. (1999), 'The learning economy, the learning firm and the learning region: a sympathetic critique of the limits to learning', *European Urban and Regional Studies*, 6(1): 59–72.

Hurley, R. F., G. T. M. Hult and G. A. Knight (2005), 'Innovativeness and capacity to innovate in a complexity of firm-level relationships: a response to Woodside (2004)', *Industrial Marketing Management*, 34(3): 281–3.

Jacobs, J. (1961), *The Death and Life of Great American Cities*, New York: Vintage Books.

Jacobs, J. (1969), *The Economy of Cities*, New York: Random House.

Jæger, B. and K. Storgaard (eds) (1997), *Telematics and Rural Development*, Nexo: Research Centre of Borholm.

Jaffe, A. B. (1989), 'Real effects of economic research', *American Economic Review*, 79(5): 957–70.

Janelle, D. G. (1969), 'Spatial reorganization: a model and a concept', *Annals of the Association of American Geographers*, 59(2): 348–64.

Jasiecki, K. (2007), 'Reform of the country possible only through social dialogue', *Dialogue*, December, pp. 61–6.

Jensen, O. B. and T. Richardson (2004), *Making European Space: Mobility, Power and Territorial Identity*, New York: Routledge.

Jessop, B. (2002), 'Liberalism, neoliberalism, and urban governance: a state-theoretical perspective', *Antipode*, 34(3): 452–72.

Jones, M. and G. MacLeod (2004), 'Regional spaces, spaces of regionalism: territory, insurgent politics and the English question', *Transactions of the Institute of British Geographers*, 29(4): 433–52.

Kanter, R. M. (1995), *World Class: Thriving Locally in the Global Economy*, New York: Simon & Schuster.

Kealey, T. (1996), *The Economic Laws of Scientific Research*, London: Macmillan.

Keil, R. (2000), 'Governance restructuring in Los Angeles and Toronto: amalgamation or secession?', *International Journal of Urban and Regional Research*, 24(4): 758–81.

Keil, R. (2002), 'Common-sense neoliberalism: progressive conservative urbanism in Toronto, Canada', *Antipode*, 34(3): 578–601.

Kline, S. J. and N. Rosenberg (1986), 'An overview of innovation', in R. Landau and N. Rosenberg (eds), *The Positive Sum Strategy: Harnessing Strategy for Economic Growth*, Washington, DC: National Academy Press, pp. 275–305.

Krugman, P. (1990), 'Increasing returns and economic geography', Working Paper no. 3275, Cambridge: NBER.

Krugman, P. (1993), 'Competitiveness – a dangerous obsession', *Foreign Affairs*, 73(2): 28–46.

Krugman, P. (1995), *Development, Geography and Economic Theory*, Cambridge, MA: MIT Press.

Krugman, P. and A. Venables (1995), 'Globalization and the inequality of nations', *Quarterly Journal of Economics*, 110: 857–9.

Lang, W. (2005), 'Knowledge spillovers in different dimensions of proximity', Paper presented at the Regional Studies Association International Conference 'Regional Growth Agendas', Aalborg, May.

Latendresse, A. (2004), 'Democracy in Montreal: one step forward, two steps back', *Canadian Dimension*, 38(5): 39–40.

Laurent, C. and I. Bowler (eds) (1997), *CAP and the Regions: Building a Multidisciplinary Framework for the Analysis of EU Agricultural Space*, Paris: INRA Editions.

Leitner, A. and E. Shepard (1997), 'Economic uncertainty, inter-urban competition and the efficacy of entrepreneurialism', in T. Hall and P. Hubbard (eds), *The Entrepreneurial City: Geographies of Politics, Regime and Representation*, London: Wiley, pp. 285–308.

Leonardi, R. (2005), *Cohesion Policy in the European Union: The Building of Europe*, Basingstoke: Palgrave.

Lovering, J. (1999), 'Theory led by policy: the inadequacies of the new regionalism (illustrated from the case of Wales)', *International Journal of Urban and Regional Research*, 23(2): 379–95.

Lund, L. (1986), 'Locating corporate R&D facilities', Conference Board Report no. 892, New York: Conference Board.

Lundvall, B. A. and B. Johnson (1994), 'The learning economy', *Journal of Industrial Studies*, 1: 23–42.

MacKinnon, D., A. Cumbers and K. Chapman (2002), 'Learning, innovation and regional development: a critical appraisal of recent debates', *Progress in Human Geography*, 26(3): 293–311.

MacLeod, G. (2002), 'From urban entrepreneurialism to a revanchist city? On the special injustices of Glasgow's renaissance', *Antipode*, 34(3): 602–24.

Maczynski, J. (1994), 'Culture and leadership styles: a comparison of Polish, Austrian and US managers', *Polish Psychological Bulletin*, 28(3): 255–67.

Malizia, E. and E. Faser (1999), *Understanding Local Economic Development*, New Brunswick: Center for Urban Policy Research.

Marshall, A. (1890), *The Principles of Economics*, London: Macmillan.

Marston, S. A. (2000), 'The social construction of scale', *Progress in Human Geography*, 24(2): 219–42.

Marston, S. A., P. Knox and D. M. Liverman (2005), *World Regions in Global Context: Peoples, Places and Environments*, New Jersey: Prentice Hall.

Martin, R. and P. Sunley (2003), 'Deconstructing clusters: chaotic concepts or policy panacea?', *Journal of Economic Geography*, 3(1): 5–35.

Maskell, P. (2001), 'Social capital, innovation and competitiveness', in S. Baron, J. Field and T. Schuller (eds), *Social Capital: Critical Perspectives*, Oxford: Oxford University Press, pp. 111–23.

Maskell, P. and G. Törnqvist (1999), *Building a Cross-border Learning Region*, Copenhagen: Handelshøjskolen, Forlag.

Matusiak, K. B. (2003), 'Business incubators in Poland', *International Journal of Entrepreneurship and Innovation Management*, 3(1/2): 87–98.

McGuirk, P. M. (1997), 'Multiscaled interpretations of urban change: the federal, the state, and the local in the Western Area Strategy of Adelaide', *Environment and Planning D: Society and Space*, 15(4): 481–98.

Meadowcroft, J. and M. Pennington (2007), *Rescuing Social Capital from Social Democracy*, London: Institute of Economic Affairs.

Meisinger, C. (2006), *EU Rural Development Policy 2007–2013*, Brussels: DG Agri, January.

Mises, L. von (1949), *Human Action: A Treatise on Economics*, New Haven, CT: Yale University Press.

Molle, W. T. M. and I. J. Boeckhout (1995), 'Economic disparity under conditions of integration: a long-term view of the economic case', *Papers in Regional Science*, 74(2): 105–23.

Morgan, K. (1997), 'The learning region: institutions, innovation and regional renewal', *Regional Studies*, 31(5): 491–503.

Moulaert, F. and F. Sekia (2003), 'Territorial innovation models: a critical survey', *Regional Studies*, 37(3): 289–302.

Munkhammar, J. (2007), *The Guide to Reform*, Stockholm: Timbro.

National Defense Research Institute (2008), *Perspectives on US Competitiveness in Science and Technology*, RAND Corporation; available at: www.rand.org/pubs/conf_proceedings/2007/RAND_CF235.pdf/.

National Electoral Office (2006), *List of Elected Mayors. Elections on 12 and 26 November 2006*; available at: www.pkw.gov.pl/gallery/57/77/57775/ML-statystyka_wojtow_wg_komitetow.pdf/.

Nonaka, I. and H. Takeuchi (1995), *The Knowledge-creating Company: How Japanese Companies Create the Dynamics of Innovation*, New York: Oxford University Press.

Nonaka, I. and R. Toyama (2002), 'A firm as dialectic being: towards a dynamic theory of the firm', *Industrial and Corporate Change*, 11(5): 995–1009.

Nonaka, I., R. Toyama and N. Konno (2000), 'SECI, Ba, and leadership: a unified model of dynamic knowledge creation', *Long Range Planning*, 33: 1–31.

OECD (1997), *Oslo Manual: Proposed Guidelines for Collecting and Interpreting Technological Innovation Data*, 2nd edn, Paris: OECD.

OECD (2001a), *Cities and Regions in the New Learning Economy, Education and Skills*, Paris: OECD.

OECD (2001b), *Information and Communication Technologies and Rural Development*, Paris: OECD.

OECD (2004), *Employment Outlook*, Paris: OECD.

OECD (2005), *Regions at a Glance*, Paris: OECD.

OECD (2006), *OECD Territorial Reviews: Newcastle in the North East, the United Kingdom*, Paris: OECD.

OECD (2008), *OECD Reviews of Tertiary Education. Poland*, Paris: OECD; available at: http://213.253.134.43/oecd/pdfs/browseit/9107091E.PDF/.

Ohmae, K. (1995), *The End of the Nation State*, New York: Free Press.

Oinas, P. and E. J. Malecki (1999), 'Spatial innovation systems', in E. J. Malecki and P. Oinas (eds), *Making Connections: Technological Learning and Regional Economic Change*, Aldershot: Ashgate, pp. 7–33.

Ostrom, E. (2005), *Understanding Institutional Diversity*, Princeton, NJ: Princeton University Press.

Paleo, I. O. and N. M. Wijnberg (2008), 'Organisational output innovativeness: a theoretical exploration, illustrated by a case of a popular music festival', *Creativity and Innovation Management*, 17(1): 3–13.

Pańków, W. and B. Gąciarz (2006), 'Polish work against the European background', *Dialog*, June, pp. 65–71.

Park, B.-G. (2003), 'Politics of scale and the globalization of the South Korean automobile industry', *Economic Geography*, 79(2): 173–94.

Parker, W. (2003), *Teaching Democracy: Unity and Diversity in Public Life*, New York: Teachers College Press.

Pastor, M., P. Dreier, E. Grigsby and M. Lopez-Garza (2000), *Regions that Work: How Cities and Suburbs Can Grow Together*, Minneapolis: University of Minnesota Press.

Peltokorpi, V., I. Nonaka and M. Kodama (2007), 'NTT DoCoMo's Launch of I-mode in the Japanese phone market: a knowledge creation perspective', *Journal of Management Studies*, 44(1): 50–72.

Polanyi, M. (1966), *The Tacit Dimension*, London: Routledge & Kegan Paul.

Porter, M. (1990), *The Competitive Advantage of Nations*, London: Macmillan.

Porter, M. (2007), 'Business and Innovation', *The Economist*, 8555, 17 November, pp. 20–21.

PRO INNO Europe (2008), *European Innovation Scoreboard 2007*; available at: www.proinno-europe.eu/.

Purcell, M. (2004), 'Regionalism and the liberal–radical divide', *Editorial Board of Antipode*, pp. 760–65.

Purcell, M. (2006), 'Urban democracy and the local trap', *Urban Studies*, 43(11): 1921–41.

Putnam, R. D. (1995), 'Bowling alone: America's declining social capital', *Journal of Democracy*, 6(1): 65–78.

Rennie, D. (2008), 'In the nick of time', *The Economist*, 8582, 31 May, pp. 3–16.

Revilla Diez, J. and M. Kiese (2006), 'Scaling innovation in South East Asia: empirical evidence from Singapore, Penang (Malaysia) and Bangkok', *Regional Studies*, 40(9): 1005–23.

Richardson, R. and V. Belt (2001), 'Saved by the bell? Call centres and economic development in less favoured regions', *Economic and Industrial Democracy*, 22(1): 67–98.

Rodrìgues-Pose, A. (2001), 'Killing economic geography with a "cultural turn" overdose', *Antipode*, 33(2): 176–82.

Rodrìgues-Pose, A. and U. Fratesi (2002), *Unbalanced Development Strategies and the Lack of Regional Convergence in the EU*, London School of Economics Research Papers in Environmental Analysis no. 76, London.

Romer, P. (1986), 'Increasing returns and long-run growth', *Journal of Political Economy*, 94(5): 1002–37.

Rusk, D. (1999), *Inside Game/Outside Game: Winning Strategies for Saving Urban America*, Washington, DC: Brookings Institute Press.

Rychly, L. and M. Vylitova (2005), *National Social Dialogue on Employment Policies in Europe*, Geneva: ILO.

Rzońca, A. and W. Wojciechowski (2008), 'How much do early retirements cost us?', Forum Obywatelskiego Rozwoju, Towarzystwo Ekonomistów Polskich, Warsaw; available at: www.for.org.pl/upload/File/raporty/Raport_0%20 kosztach_emerytur_FINAL.pdf/.

Santos, I. (2008), 'Is structural spending on solid foundations?', *Bruguel Policy Brief*, 2008/02, Brussels: Bruguel.

Sapir, A., P. Aghion, G. Bertola, M. Hellwig, J. Pisani-Ferry, D. Rosati, J. Viñals and H. Wallace (2004), *An Agenda for a Growing Europe. The Sapir Report*, New York: Oxford University Press.

Sassen, S. (1993), *Cities in the World Economy*, London: Sage.

Saxenian, A. (1994), *Regional Advantage: Culture and Competition in Silicon Valley and Route 128*, Cambridge, MA: Harvard University Press.

Schmied, D. (ed.) (2002), *Winning and Losing: The Changing Geography of Europe's Rural Areas*, Aldershot: Ashgate.

Schnabel, C. and J. Wagner (2007), 'Union density and determinants of union membership in 18 EU countries: evidence from micro data', *Industrial Relations*, 38(1): 5–32.

Scott, A. J. (1996), 'Regional motors of the global economy', *Futures*, 28(5): 391–411.

Scott, A. J. (1998), *Regions and the World Economy*, Oxford: Oxford University Press.

Scott, S. G. and R. A. Bruce (1994), 'Determinants of innovative behaviour: a path model of innovation in the workplace', *Academy of Management Journal*, 37(3): 580–607.

Shanghai Jiao Tong University (2008), *Academic Ranking of World Universities 2007*; available at: www.arwu.org/rank/2007/ranking2007.htm/.

Shucksmith, M., K. Thomson and D. Roberts (eds) (2005), *CAP and the Regions: Territorial Impact of Common Agricultural Policy*, Wallingford: CAB International.

Siebert, W. S. (2005) 'Labour market regulation: some comparative lessons', *Economic Affairs*, 25(3): 3–10.

Siegele, L. (2006), 'Waiting for a wunder', *The Economist*, 8464, 11 February, pp. 3–20.

Siemianowicz, J. (2006), 'Transformation, integration and then?', *International Journal of Entrepreneurship and Innovation Management*, 6(1/2): 102–9.

Simmie, J. (1997), *Innovation, Networks and Learning Regions? Regional Policy and Development*, London: Jessica Kingsley Publishers/RSA.

Simmie, J. (2003), 'Innovation and urban regions as national and international nodes for the transfer and sharing of knowledge', *Regional Studies*, 37(6/7): 607–20.

Smith, D. B. (2006), *Living with Leviathan*, London: Institute of Economic Affairs.

Smith, K. (2000), *What Is the 'Knowledge Economy'? Knowledge-intensive Industries and Distributed Knowledge Bases*, Luxembourg: CORDIS.

Storper, M. (1997), *The Regional World, Territorial Development in a Global Economy*, New York: Guildford Press.

Swyngedouw, E. (1989), 'The heart of the place: the resurrection of locality in an age of hyperspace', *Geografiska Annaler B*, 21: 31–42.

Swyngedouw, E. (1997), 'Neither global nor local: "glocalization" and the politics of scale', in K. Cox (ed.), *Spaces of Globalisation: Reasserting the Power of the Local*, New York: Guildford Press, pp. 137–66.

Szomburg, J. (ed.) (2001), *State Regional Policy amid Institutional-Regulatory Complexities*, Gdańsk: IbnGR.

Sztompka, P. (2002), *Sociology*, Kraków: Znak.

Tarditi, S. and G. Zanias (2001), 'Common Agricultural Policy', in R. Hal, A. Smith and L. Tsoukalis (eds), *Competitiveness and Cohesion in EU Policies*, Oxford: Oxford University Press, pp. 179–216.

Teather, R. (2006), *The Benefits of Tax Competition*, Hobart Paper 153, London: Institute of Economic Affairs.

Te Velde, R. A. (1999), 'Market for knowledge: where do minds meet?', Paper presented at the EAPPE conference, November, Prague.

Tischner, J. (1992), *The Ethics of Solidarity. Homo sovieticus*, Kraków: Znak.

Tittenbrun, J. (1992) *The Collapse of Real Socialism in Poland*, Poznań: Rebis.

Torrance, M. I. (2008), 'Urban infrastructure as networked financial products', *International Journal of Urban and Regional Research*, 32(1): 1–21.

Trigilia, C. (2001), 'Social capital and local development', *European Journal of Social Theory*, 4(4): 427–42.

Tura, T. and V. Harmaamkorpi (2005), 'Social capital in building regional innovative capability', *Regional Studies*, 39(8): 1111–25.

Utterback, J. M. (1994), *Mastering the Dynamics of Innovation*, Boston, MA: Harvard Business School Press.

Wałęsa, L. (1990), *The Road of Hope*, 2nd edn, Kraków: Znak.

Wolfe, D. A. and M. S. Gertler (2004), 'Clusters from the inside and out: local dynamics and global linkages', *Urban Studies*, 41(5/6): 1071–93.

Wood, S. (1999), 'HRM and performance', *International Journal of Management Reviews*, 1(4): 387–413.

Woodall, P. (2000), 'Untangling e-conomics', *The Economist*, 8193, 23 September, pp. 5–44.

World Bank (2008), *Doing Business 2009*; available at: www.doingbusiness.org/economyrankings/.

World Economic Forum (2008a), *Global Competitiveness Index 2007/2008*; available at: *www.gcr.weforum.org/*.

World Economic Forum (2008b), *Travel and Tourism Competitiveness Report 2008*; available at: www.weforum.org/en/initiatives/gcp/TravelandTourismReport/index.htm/.

Zielonka, J. (2001), 'How new enlarged borders will reshape the European Union', *Journal of Common Market Studies*, 39(3): 507–36.

Zielonka, J. and A. Krok-Paszkowska (2004), 'Poland's road to the European Union', *Journal of European Integration History*, 10(2): 7–24.

Zientara, P. (2006a), 'Employment protection legislation and the growth of the service sector in the European Union', *Economic Affairs*, 26(4): 46–52.

Zientara, P. (2006b), 'The pros and cons of Poland's early euro membership', *Wspólnoty Europejskie*, 11, Warsaw: Foreign Trade Research Institute, pp. 3–10.

Zientara, P. (2007), 'How trade unions are a roadblock to Poland's economic renaissance', *Economic Affairs*, 27(1): 44–51.

Zientara, P. (2008a), 'A report on the Polish labour market: an insider-outsider system', *Industrial Relations: A Journal of Economy & Society*, 47(3): 419–29.

Zientara, P. (2008b), 'Polish regions in the age of a knowledge-based economy', *International Journal of Urban and Regional Research*, 32(1): 65–80.

Zięba, S. and A. Kowalski (eds) (2007), *Development of Agriculture, Food Production and Polish Rural Areas in the EU*, Warsaw: Almamer i Instytut Ekonomiki Rolnictwa i Gospodarki Żywnościowej – Państwowy Instytut Badawczy.

Zybała, A. (2006), 'Power of dialogue', *Dialog*, July, pp. 54–8.

Zybertowicz, A. and M. Spławski (2006), 'Is social dialogue an alien organism in Polish social life?', *Dialog*, June, pp. 16–22.

ABOUT THE IEA

The Institute is a research and educational charity (No. CC 235 351), limited by guarantee. Its mission is to improve understanding of the fundamental institutions of a free society by analysing and expounding the role of markets in solving economic and social problems.

The IEA achieves its mission by:

- a high-quality publishing programme
- conferences, seminars, lectures and other events
- outreach to school and college students
- brokering media introductions and appearances

The IEA, which was established in 1955 by the late Sir Antony Fisher, is an educational charity, not a political organisation. It is independent of any political party or group and does not carry on activities intended to affect support for any political party or candidate in any election or referendum, or at any other time. It is financed by sales of publications, conference fees and voluntary donations.

In addition to its main series of publications the IEA also publishes a quarterly journal, *Economic Affairs*.

The IEA is aided in its work by a distinguished international Academic Advisory Council and an eminent panel of Honorary Fellows. Together with other academics, they review prospective IEA publications, their comments being passed on anonymously to authors. All IEA papers are therefore subject to the same rigorous independent refereeing process as used by leading academic journals.

IEA publications enjoy widespread classroom use and course adoptions in schools and universities. They are also sold throughout the world and often translated/reprinted.

Since 1974 the IEA has helped to create a worldwide network of 100 similar institutions in over 70 countries. They are all independent but share the IEA's mission.

Views expressed in the IEA's publications are those of the authors, not those of the Institute (which has no corporate view), its Managing Trustees, Academic Advisory Council members or senior staff.

Members of the Institute's Academic Advisory Council, Honorary Fellows, Trustees and Staff are listed on the following page.

The Institute gratefully acknowledges financial support for its publications programme and other work from a generous benefaction by the late Alec and Beryl Warren.

The Institute of Economic Affairs
2 Lord North Street, Westminster, London SW1P 3LB
Tel: 020 7799 8900
Fax: 020 7799 2137
Email: iea@iea.org.uk
Internet: iea.org.uk

Other papers recently published by the IEA include:

A Market in Airport Slots
Keith Boyfield (editor), David Starkie, Tom Bass & Barry Humphreys
Readings 56; ISBN 0 255 36505 5; £10.00

Money, Inflation and the Constitutional Position of the Central Bank
Milton Friedman & Charles A. E. Goodhart
Readings 57; ISBN 0 255 36538 1; £10.00

railway.com
Parallels between the Early British Railways and the ICT Revolution
Robert C. B. Miller
Research Monograph 57; ISBN 0 255 36534 9; £12.50

The Regulation of Financial Markets
Edited by Philip Booth & David Currie
Readings 58; ISBN 0 255 36551 9; £12.50

Climate Alarmism Reconsidered
Robert L. Bradley Jr
Hobart Paper 146; ISBN 0 255 36541 1; £12.50

Government Failure: E. G. West on Education
Edited by James Tooley & James Stanfield
Occasional Paper 130; ISBN 0 255 36552 7; £12.50

Corporate Governance: Accountability in the Marketplace
Elaine Sternberg
Second edition
Hobart Paper 147; ISBN 0 255 36542 x; £12.50

The Land Use Planning System
Evaluating Options for Reform
John Corkindale
Hobart Paper 148; ISBN 0 255 36550 0; £10.00

Economy and Virtue
Essays on the Theme of Markets and Morality
Edited by Dennis O'Keeffe
Readings 59; ISBN 0 255 36504 7; £12.50

Free Markets Under Siege
Cartels, Politics and Social Welfare
Richard A. Epstein
Occasional Paper 132; ISBN 0 255 36553 5; £10.00

Unshackling Accountants
D. R. Myddelton
Hobart Paper 149; ISBN 0 255 36559 4; £12.50

The Euro as Politics
Pedro Schwartz
Research Monograph 58; ISBN 0 255 36535 7; £12.50

Pricing Our Roads
Vision and Reality
Stephen Glaister & Daniel J. Graham
Research Monograph 59; ISBN 0 255 36562 4; £10.00

The Role of Business in the Modern World
Progress, Pressures, and Prospects for the Market Economy
David Henderson
Hobart Paper 150; ISBN 0 255 36548 9; £12.50

Public Service Broadcasting Without the BBC?
Alan Peacock
Occasional Paper 133; ISBN 0 255 36565 9; £10.00

The ECB and the Euro: the First Five Years
Otmar Issing
Occasional Paper 134; ISBN 0 255 36555 1; £10.00

Towards a Liberal Utopia?
Edited by Philip Booth
Hobart Paperback 32; ISBN 0 255 36563 2; £15.00

The Way Out of the Pensions Quagmire
Philip Booth & Deborah Cooper
Research Monograph 60; ISBN 0 255 36517 9; £12.50

Black Wednesday
A Re-examination of Britain's Experience in the Exchange Rate Mechanism
Alan Budd
Occasional Paper 135; ISBN 0 255 36566 7; £7.50

Crime: Economic Incentives and Social Networks
Paul Ormerod
Hobart Paper 151; ISBN 0 255 36554 3; £10.00

The Road to Serfdom *with* **The Intellectuals and Socialism**
Friedrich A. Hayek
Occasional Paper 136; ISBN 0 255 36576 4; £10.00

Money and Asset Prices in Boom and Bust
Tim Congdon
Hobart Paper 152; ISBN 0 255 36570 5; £10.00

The Dangers of Bus Re-regulation
and Other Perspectives on Markets in Transport
John Hibbs et al.
Occasional Paper 137; ISBN 0 255 36572 1; £10.00

The New Rural Economy
Change, Dynamism and Government Policy
Berkeley Hill et al.
Occasional Paper 138; ISBN 0 255 36546 2; £15.00

The Benefits of Tax Competition
Richard Teather
Hobart Paper 153; ISBN 0 255 36569 1; £12.50

Wheels of Fortune
Self-funding Infrastructure and the Free Market Case for a Land Tax
Fred Harrison
Hobart Paper 154; ISBN 0 255 36589 6; £12.50

Were 364 Economists All Wrong?
Edited by Philip Booth
Readings 60; ISBN 978 0 255 36588 8; £10.00

Europe After the 'No' Votes
Mapping a New Economic Path
Patrick A. Messerlin
Occasional Paper 139; ISBN 978 0 255 36580 2; £10.00

The Railways, the Market and the Government
John Hibbs et al.
Readings 61; ISBN 978 0 255 36567 3; £12.50

Corruption: The World's Big C
Cases, Causes, Consequences, Cures
Ian Senior
Research Monograph 61; ISBN 978 0 255 36571 0; £12.50

Choice and the End of Social Housing
Peter King
Hobart Paper 155; ISBN 978 0 255 36568 0; £10.00

Sir Humphrey's Legacy
Facing Up to the Cost of Public Sector Pensions
Neil Record
Hobart Paper 156; ISBN 978 0 255 36578 9; £10.00

The Economics of Law
Cento Veljanovski
Second edition
Hobart Paper 157; ISBN 978 0 255 36561 1; £12.50

Living with Leviathan
Public Spending, Taxes and Economic Performance
David B. Smith
Hobart Paper 158; ISBN 978 0 255 36579 6; £12.50

The Vote Motive
Gordon Tullock
New edition
Hobart Paperback 33; ISBN 978 0 255 36577 2; £10.00

Waging the War of Ideas
John Blundell
Third edition
Occasional Paper 131; ISBN 978 0 255 36606 9; £12.50

The War Between the State and the Family
How Government Divides and Impoverishes
Patricia Morgan
Hobart Paper 159; ISBN 978 0 255 36596 3; £10.00

Capitalism – A Condensed Version
Arthur Seldon
Occasional Paper 140; ISBN 978 0 255 36598 7; £7.50

Catholic Social Teaching and the Market Economy
Edited by Philip Booth
Hobart Paperback 34; ISBN 978 0 255 36581 9; £15.00

Adam Smith – A Primer
Eamonn Butler
Occasional Paper 141; ISBN 978 0 255 36608 3; £7.50

Happiness, Economics and Public Policy
Helen Johns & Paul Ormerod
Research Monograph 62; ISBN 978 0 255 36600 7; £10.00

They Meant Well
Government Project Disasters
D. R. Myddelton
Hobart Paper 160; ISBN 978 0 255 36601 4; £12.50

Rescuing Social Capital from Social Democracy
John Meadowcroft & Mark Pennington
Hobart Paper 161; ISBN 978 0 255 36592 5; £10.00

Paths to Property
Approaches to Institutional Change in International Development
Karol Boudreaux & Paul Dragos Aligica
Hobart Paper 162; ISBN 978 0 255 36582 6; £10.00

Prohibitions
Edited by John Meadowcroft
Hobart Paperback 35; ISBN 978 0 255 36585 7; £15.00

Trade Policy, New Century
The WTO, FTAs and Asia Rising
Razeen Sally
Hobart Paper 163; ISBN 978 0 255 36544 4; £12.50

Sixty Years On – Who Cares for the NHS?
Helen Evans
Research Monograph 63; ISBN 978 0 255 36611 3; £10.00

Taming Leviathan
Waging the War of Ideas Around the World
Edited by Colleen Dyble
Occasional Paper 142; ISBN 978 0 255 36607 6; £12.50

The Legal Foundations of Free Markets
Edited by Stephen F. Copp
Hobart Paperback 36; ISBN 978 0 255 36591 8; £15.00

Climate Change Policy: Challenging the Activists
Edited by Colin Robinson
Readings 62; ISBN 978 0 255 36595 6; £10.00

Should We Mind the Gap?
Gender Pay Differentials and Public Policy
J. R. Shackleton
Hobart Paper 164; ISBN 978 0 255 36604 5; £10.00

Pension Provision: Government Failure Around the World
Edited by Philip Booth et al.
Readings 63; ISBN 978 0 255 36602 1; £15.00

Other IEA publications

Comprehensive information on other publications and the wider work of the IEA can be found at www.iea.org.uk. To order any publication please see below.

Personal customers

Orders from personal customers should be directed to the IEA:
Bob Layson
IEA
2 Lord North Street
FREEPOST LON10168
London SW1P 3YZ
Tel: 020 7799 8909. Fax: 020 7799 2137
Email: blayson@iea.org.uk

Trade customers

All orders from the book trade should be directed to the IEA's distributor:
Gazelle Book Services Ltd (IEA Orders)
FREEPOST RLYS-EAHU-YSCZ
White Cross Mills
Hightown
Lancaster LA1 4XS
Tel: 01524 68765, Fax: 01524 53232
Email: sales@gazellebooks.co.uk

IEA subscriptions

The IEA also offers a subscription service to its publications. For a single annual payment (currently £42.00 in the UK), subscribers receive every monograph the IEA publishes. For more information please contact:
Adam Myers
Subscriptions
IEA
2 Lord North Street
FREEPOST LON10168
London SW1P 3YZ
Tel: 020 7799 8920, Fax: 020 7799 2137
Email: amyers@iea.org.uk